A Turning Point in Teacher Education

A Turning Point in Teacher Education

A Time for Resistance, Reflection, and Change

James D. Kirylo
Jerry Aldridge

ROWMAN & LITTLEFIELD
Lanham • Boulder • New York • London

Published by Rowman & Littlefield
An imprint of The Rowman & Littlefield Publishing Group, Inc.
4501 Forbes Boulevard, Suite 200, Lanham, Maryland 20706
www.rowman.com

6 Tinworth Street, London SE11 5AL, United Kingdom

Copyright © 2019 by James D. Kirylo and Jerry Aldridge

All rights reserved. No part of this book may be reproduced in any form or by any electronic or mechanical means, including information storage and retrieval systems, without written permission from the publisher, except by a reviewer who may quote passages in a review.

British Library Cataloguing in Publication Information Available

Library of Congress Cataloging-in-Publication Data

Names: Kirylo, James D., author. | Aldridge, Jerry, author.
Title: A turning point in teacher education : a time for resistance, reflection, and change / James D. Kirylo and Jerry Aldridge.
Description: Lanham, Maryland : Rowman & Littlefield, [2019] | Includes bibliographical references and index.
Identifiers: LCCN 2018046489 (print) | LCCN 2018053988 (ebook) | ISBN 9781475827071 (Electronic) | ISBN 9781475827057 (cloth : alk. paper) | ISBN 9781475827064 (pbk. : alk. paper)
Subjects: LCSH: Teachers—Training of. | Educational change. | Education and state. | Education—Aims and objectives.
Classification: LCC LB1707 (ebook) | LCC LB1707 .K57 2019 (print) | DDC 370.71/1—23
LC record available at https://lccn.loc.gov/2018046489

∞™ The paper used in this publication meets the minimum requirements of American National Standard for Information Sciences—Permanence of Paper for Printed Library Materials, ANSI/NISO Z39.48-1992.

Printed in the United States of America

Contents

Acknowledgments		vii
Introduction: What Is Happening with Teacher Education?		ix

Part I: Activism Matters

1 Turning Points — 3

Part II: The Hijacking of the Education Narrative

2 Reform, Accountability, and Compromising K–12 Education — 21
3 Neoliberalism: A Systematic Effort to Privatize — 27
4 Working to Eliminate Traditional Teacher Education Programs — 31

Part III: Teacher Education and the Politics Within

5 A Rocky Historical Road toward Teacher Education — 39
6 Sameness versus Difference: Is Teacher Education Clear about Faculty Expectations? — 45
7 Sameness versus Difference: Is Teacher Education Fair about Compensation and the Hiring Process? — 49
8 The Macro versus Micro Challenge — 53
9 Two-Stepping among Colleges of Education, Accrediting Agencies, and State Departments of Education — 57
10 Quantity versus Quality in Accepting Teacher Candidates — 61

Part IV: The Question of What and How to Teach

11 The Relationship between Curriculum and Instruction — 65

12	Models, Approaches, and Frameworks: What's the Difference?	69
13	How Should We Teach?: Transmission, Transaction, or Transformation	73
14	Should We Emphasize Universal Human Development or Diversity?	79
15	The Question of Online Delivery Systems in Teacher Education	89

Part V: Teacher Education and Moving Forward

| 16 | Realize the Distraction in Order to Move Forward | 97 |
| 17 | In Need of a "Flexner-Like" Moment in Teacher Education | 101 |

References	107
Index	121
About the Authors	129

Acknowledgments

Thank you, Tom Koerner, vice president and publisher at Rowman & Littlefield, for having the vision for this book. Also, within Rowman & Littlefield, many thanks to Carlie Wall and Melissa McNitt for your guidance to bring this book to completion. Thank you, Jerry Aldridge, for your time, energy, and expertise. Working on this book has been a rewarding experience. Thank you, John Fischetti, for all the conversations we have had over the years. You have keen insight. And most importantly, many thanks to my wife, Anette, who has been patient, supportive, and encouraging as I worked furiously toward the end of this project to meet our deadline. I am most grateful to you and our two wonderful sons, Antonio and Alexander. Always. Blessed.

• • •

Jerry dedicates this book to the memory of his parents, J. Titus Aldridge and Winnie Aldridge, as well as his beloved aunt, Gay Nell Trawick. He would also like to gratefully acknowledge the support of friends, family, and colleagues including Jessica Capp, Susan Sudduth, Chao Dong, Lois and Paul Christensen, Jennifer L. Kilgo, Linda Kay Emfinger, C. Michael Baker, Patricia Kuby, Candace Kuby, Grace Jepkemboi, Isabel Killoren, Willis Walter, Vincent Ng, Michael L. Herrington, Catherine Kirkpatrick, Don Medina, Ricky Aman, Rozz Embi, and Javier Mondragon, as well as his mentors, Milly Cowles, Robert J. Canady, Tommy Russell, Aver Rumley, Catherine Johnston, and Marion Nissen. Finally, he would like to thank James D. Kirylo for the opportunity to work with him. For the opportunity to be a part of this manuscript, Jerry gives gratitude to God.

Introduction

What Is Happening with Teacher Education?

Since teacher education became a formal field of study in the 1800s under the work of Horace Mann, it has undergone a rocky history that has endured a continuous wave of criticism peppered with the ever-present hovering of those delegitimizing its relevance. Yet something is happening with teacher education that is unprecedented.

While this history of teacher education criticism is not a new phenomenon, it is entering an unprecedented space in which not only is the formal study of education being undermined but also the very fabric of the public square is in the process of being weakened. Somehow the disruptive nature of economic change, social upheaval, and globalization are put upon the backs of teachers, particularly public school teachers.

Largely driven by free market advocates promoting competition over a growing knowledge base, the advancing of this competition pushes educational, social, health-care, and civic systems that inherently leave some in and others out—further alienating the disenfranchised.

In other words, a neoliberal agenda has been hard at work to advance privatization and outsourcing anything from government that is possible, with no interest in the common good.[1] Within that mix, teacher education is caught in the larger conversation, a conversation that simultaneously leans toward minimizing critical thought and is fixated on teacher training, expediency, and mindless methodological indoctrination.

As U.S. secretary of education Betsy DeVos exclaimed in 2017, on her first school visit in her new post, "Teachers are waiting to be told what they have to do" (Darville, 2017). Her patronizing remarks of teachers are palpable.

Likewise, in 2002 in a report by then secretary of education Rodney Paige, in which he, on one hand, was pushing for "highly qualified" teachers under the No Child Left Behind (NCLB) Act, yet was quick to castigate teacher education programs and question their significance, and maligned what he considered burdensome requirements, while touting fast-track programs toward certification. A focus on fast-track programs minimizes the importance of educational theory, philosophies of education, and pedagogy, and promotes the idea that the craft of teaching is learned while on the job (U.S. Department of Education, 2002).[2]

Indeed, the advent of well-funded, fast-track teacher "training" programs such as Teach for America (TFA), Teach for All (an offshoot of TFA), the New Teacher Project, and other related programs—which possess cool, crisp commercialized websites and well-oiled recruiting mechanisms, and largely operate on the faulty premise that traditional university teacher education programs are not doing a good job—are working overtime to delegitimize traditional teacher education programs.

In other words, these fast-track programs recruit itinerants with college degrees who generally go into hard-to-staff teaching situations where some quit before they even start; recruit still others who don't even complete their two-year commitment; and recruit many who, once the two-year stint is up, leave teaching in the rearview mirror. In short, "teachers with little preparation tend to leave at rates two to three times as high as those who have had a comprehensive preparation before they enter" (Sutcher, Darling-Hammond, & Carver-Thomas, 2016, p. 4).

Where Paige and his associates worked hard to diminish the place of traditional teacher education well over a decade ago, the National Council on Teacher Quality (NCTQ) picked up the mantle with aiding and abetting the legitimacy of fast-track teacher training programs. That is, NCTQ clearly possesses a fundamental distain for traditional teacher education programs, taking every opportunity to rate them low through their partnership with the *U.S. News & World Report* annual edition that misleadingly reports the rankings of schools of education from around the country (Ravitch, 2012a, 2017).

In addition to the assault on teacher education from outside forces, many teacher education programs across the country are working to undercut themselves within by being co-opted by such programs as the National Institute for Excellence in Teaching (NIET), a Lowell Milken education corporate enterprise. Emphasizing a prescriptive "training" model through its System for Teacher and Student Advancement (TAP) and Best Practices Center (BPC) template, and driven by "data-driven" instruction, NIET cleverly sucks in many colleges of education as the host to further their privatized program (see, e.g., *TTU*, 2015).

The latter, therefore, translates into teacher educators being forced to undergo training in order to conform, which not ironically undermines the value of tenure, dismisses the notion of academic freedom, and ultimately works to defund traditional teacher education programs. In addition to NIET, it is no coincidence that other similar types of programs have emerged over the past several years (e.g., Relay Graduate School, Teacher Preparation Analytics, TPA, TPI-US, and others).

To get to the place where we are today has been a decades-long unfolding process, one that has as its aim to ultimately eradicate traditional teacher education programs. That is a very bad thing. Yet are we suggesting that traditional teacher education programs have no room for improvement or should be resistant to change? Of course not. Teacher education has a long history of its own internal struggles.

For example, the status, funding sources, and expectations for Research I or flagship universities can be quite different from regional universities settings, all of which interconnects hiring practices and the political landmine relative to concepts intersecting research, service, teaching load, and tenure and promotion.

Then there is the tension of whether teacher educators should prepare teacher candidates at the macro level (i.e., from a more global or national perspective) or from a micro level (i.e., from a more local school district, community, or individual classroom perspective) or from both perspectives. And if so from the latter, how is that tension negotiated?

In addition to the above, teacher education programs have had a long history of an often-tenuous relationship coexisting with accrediting agencies and state departments of education. That is, in many instances programs often find themselves in a defensive posture, yet continuously in a subordinate role, to "please" accrediting agencies and state departments of education.

Particularly with the latter, many who oversee the department—not as a matter of haughtiness but as a matter of fact—are less experienced, are less knowledgeable, and possess less education than teacher educators but have no compunction in throwing their weight around to dictate the direction of teacher education. With respect to the former, it is not uncommon for teacher educators to be so focused on meeting the "standards" of the accrediting agencies that they diminish their own professionalism, expertise, authenticity, and what actually may be relevant in their respective settings.

Then there is the question of the quantity-versus-quality conundrum when it comes to teacher education. That is, as states defund higher education and erringly continue to move down the road to a tuition-driven model of funding, teacher education (as in the case of other university schools and colleges) has to grapple with how to sift through the quantity of students to admit and retain in order to meet university tuition-driven funding paradigms juxtaposed to the acceptance of the quality of the potential students that would best represent respective programs.

Finally, teacher education must always reflect on their mission and focus on how to best prepare teacher candidates with respect to disposition, theoretical and philosophical positioning, content knowledge, the meaning and intent of curriculum, and instructional approaches. Indeed, that is their job, which is inherently political.

TWO FORCES AT WORK

To that collective end, there exists a juxtaposition between two broad forces at work impacting teacher education. First, there is what we are characterizing as the external forces, which is the continuous wave of the promotion of fast-track teacher training, largely led by those with a neoliberal worldview coupled with deep pockets, looking to ultimately dismantle traditional teacher education programs. In short, teacher "education" is viewed as teacher "training," which does not necessitate one having to go through a teacher education program as a formal field of study.

Second, there is what we are characterizing as internal forces, whereby teacher education within itself continues to struggle with its identity, power, and influence. On one hand, with privatized dollars dangling with set conditions, revenue-strapped teacher education programs pounce, resulting in compromising their autonomy, expertise, and identity.

On the other hand, they internally grapple with issues relative to tenure, promotion, expectations, theoretical, curricula, and instructional frameworks coupled with the dynamics of dealing with accrediting and state department agencies, all of which can create great conflict, discord, and inconsistencies among programs.

With the interfacing of these two forces, what we are portending here is that we have reached a climax point, a turning point in teacher education, whereby we must work—Freirean[3] in spirit—to simultaneously denounce those external forces that are laboring to undermine the professionalization of what it takes and means to be a teacher, and also resist those internal forces that look to teacher educators themselves who contribute to their own marginalization in thought, practice and policy, and work to announce the furthering of what should be.

In other words, the purpose of this book is to magnify and add to the existing sounding bells of resistance when it comes to the external and internal forces that work to undermine teacher education. While we are not claiming to have all the answers, nor are we here with any sort of "prescriptions," we do ask the questions, questions that we all need to answer relative to our particular settings and realities.

In the final analysis, teacher education must be clear about its identity, power, and influence, and mindful of the various forces at work in which to negotiate as we now move into the middle of the 21st century.

OVERVIEW OF BOOK

This book is divided into three broad parts. In the first part of the book we discuss how throughout the history of education there has always been some kind of triggering event, experience, or circumstance that has prompted individuals to emerge and respond to change the course of education. We discuss the work of a handful of individuals who, through their work and activism, have historically turned the direction of education with respect to pedagogy, curriculum, and policy.

Corporate reformers, in a deliberate, evolving process, have worked for the last 35 years to rearrange education in their own image. Yet we believe these reform efforts or these external forces have led us down the road to failed practices and policies, which we discuss in the second part of the book. In the third part of the book we spend a good amount of time discussing those internal forces that teacher education programs must grapple with in order to arrive at working solutions for more effective and efficient work.

Finally, in the fourth part of the book we argue that teacher education in the collective is in need of a "Flexner-like" moment. This moment emerges from the same line of thinking that drove Abraham Flexner, who led the effort regarding the momentous reformation of the medical profession in the United States and Canada in the early 1900s to earn the respect it rightly deserves to this day. In that light and in parallel fashion, the time is now once and for all for teacher education to be firmly planted on that road of respect, emphasis, and importance.

TARGETED AUDIENCE

The intended audience for this book is varied. Of course, teacher educators and pre-K–12 educators are a natural audience who would find interest in this text. In particular, teacher educators would find this text a good resource for any number of classes in curriculum and pedagogy, educational administration, and policy. Moreover, as we continue our journey into the 21st century, policy makers would certainly have interest in this text, along with still others who have a general interest in the practices, trends, and policies that drive education.

NOTES

1. While neoliberalism will be further discussed in chapter 3, in short, it is an ideology that is driven by competition, individualism, and consumerism in which an economic system is propelled by privatization, ultimately working to dismantle the public square (Kirylo, 2016a).

2. This was the same Rodney Paige who was superintendent of the Houston Independent School District in Texas, in which the "Texas Miracle" occurred with a grand spike upward of test scores. It was later revealed that all sorts of irregularities occurred during the testing process. Yet, Paige was still appointed secretary of education under the George W. Bush administration from which he led the charge of NCLB, which now most people both in and out of education have declared a failure. It is disturbing enough that there are many who promote fast-track programs toward teacher certification and sending underprepared teacher candidates in the classroom to continue their learning on the job, generally at the expense of children who come from poverty, but, as Darling-Hammond (2006) argues, "inadequate preparation also increases teacher attrition, which exacerbates the revolving door that contributes to teacher shortages" (p. 14).

3. Paulo Freire (1921–1997), one of the most important educators of our time, contends that in situations of injustice or wrongness, we must simultaneously activate our voices in denouncing unjust structures, policies, and practices, and announce a better way of doing things that is just, right, and ethical. As Freire (1997) puts it, "I cannot permit myself to be a mere spectator. On the contrary, I must demand my place in the process of change" (p. 129).

I
ACTIVISM MATTERS

• *1* •

Turning Points

$\mathcal{R}$ecorded history is filled with accounts of people who have emerged to the forefront as a result of their efforts to change the course of history. For example, consider Johannes Gutenberg (ca. 1395–1468) who developed a movable type of printing press, which enabled news, books, and religious texts to be produced faster and in greater volume, resulting in the exponential expanse of learning among the populace across Europe and beyond; or realize the drive of Susan B. Anthony (1820–1906), along with Elizabeth Cady Stanton (1815–1902), who were not only active abolitionists but also prominent leaders for the rights of women, including the right to vote.

Moreover, contemplate the genius of George Washington Carver (ca. early 1860s–1940s) who, among other agricultural and medical advancements, introduced to the world the multiple values of the peanut; ponder the adventurous spirit of Orville (1871–1948) and Wilbur (1867–1912) Wright (aka the "Wright brothers") who are credited with successfully flying the first airplane, leading us to where we are with prolific advancement in aviation; and think about the political, religious, and socially decisive activism of Martin Luther King Jr. (1929–1968) who, along with a dedicated following, profoundly changed the course of civil rights of African Americans and other minority groups in the United States, and had a worldwide impact on liberation movements.

Finally, mull over the focus of Nelson Mandela (1918–2013) who, despite spending 27 years in prison for his political activism, inspirationally led the effort to end apartheid in South Africa and went on to become that country's first Black president; reflect on the remarkable courage of the unknown man (aka the "tank man") in a white shirt and black pants who stood in protest in front of a line of tanks at Tiananmen Square in 1989, thrusting his singular iconic act of resistance to oppression as a profound inspiration for resistance efforts around the world; and last, consider the resolve of Oprah Winfrey (1954–) who, born in poverty and abused as a child, rose to the top of the television world, contemporarily becoming one of the most influential women in the world with her philanthropy work and business ventures.

Each of the highlighted individuals is representative of the hundreds and thousands of men and women—heroically known and unknown—who through their ingenuity, activism, involvement, and desire for a better world dynamically responded to a need, to an injustice, or even to an active curiosity, steering them to turn the trajectory of history in some way.[1]

Likewise, as is the case of the collective latter and responding to misdirected, faulty, or unjust practices, there have been numerous individuals who have notably turned the direction of education in some historical way. The following highlighted individuals, of course, are simply a small sampling of countless people who have shaped the history of education.

SOCRATES (CA. 469–399 BCE)

When we think of the formal recording of the notion of critical thinking, we can go as far back to Socrates who is contemporarily recognized for a pedagogical approach that is referred to as the Socratic method. That is, Socrates incorporated a methodology that was dialectical in nature, simultaneously questioning assumptions or views that one may hold while making clear it was not him (or the teacher, as it were) that was full of knowledge. Indeed, through Plato's *Apology*, it is claimed that Socrates was to have declared, "I know that I know nothing," paradoxical in nature as sometimes is the case with Socratic thought.

Through a process of questioning, students in the Socratic method draw from their own experience, yet are challenged to poke holes in the relevant data/information they have, where that data was garnered, how that data was analyzed, and how the implications are reasoned. In short, through a disciplined process, the Socratic method draws students in, in order to critically think for themselves to better understand a problem, dilemma, or challenge (Paul & Elder, 1997; Webb, Metha, & Jordan, 2007).

In other words, critical thinking is fundamentally a process that thoughtfully questions assumptions and information of all sorts in order to make sense, understand, or even rebuff those assumptions or information. In that line of reasoned thought processes, students therefore come to learn and discover on their own. This pedagogical process was different to the approach taken by the sophists or the professional teachers of ancient Greece, who generally saw their task as to transmit knowledge to their pupils. Indeed, Socrates challenged his contemporaries, which not only drew to him quite a following among the youth but also led him to become a threat to the establishment, landing him in an Athenian court for impiety and corrupting the mind of the youth.

Socrates, through cross-examination, suggested it an interesting phenomenon that the prosecutor, Meletus, believed that while the assemblymen, councilmen, and jurors of Athens all worked to correctly educate the youth, it was Socrates *alone* who worked to corrupt them. Socrates was not greatly intimidated by his accusers and was, paradoxically, claiming to the court that most Athenians in charge of educating the youth were in fact doing a poor job with such a task. Socrates went on to famously argue to the court that he was simply a "gadfly" who aims to wake up the polis that had become sluggish, despite the swatting of the polis to shut him down (Ober, 2003).

As history records, Socrates was sent to prison and sentenced to death. And though there were followers who provided an avenue for him to escape prison, Socrates refused and met his fate by drinking the prescribed hemlock. Now referred to as the "father" of Western philosophy, Socrates has significantly contributed to how we approach the process of teaching and learning.

JEAN-JACQUES ROUSSEAU (1712–1778)

Rousseau's political philosophy had an impact on the thinking of his followers who saw a feudal system keeping masses of people in a subjected state, thus stoking the flames of the French Revolution. But like John Locke, he importantly contributed to the unfolding of developmental psychology, as both were influenced by John Amos Comenius (1592–1670) who argued that children learned differently than adults, implying that childhood was a unique stage of life in which learning occurs through experience.[2] And while Rousseau was in agreement with Locke that children are different from adults, he parts ways with him in that he had no faith in the social environment, as he lays out in his classic work *Emile* (Crain, 2000).

So, for Rousseau, children were born pure, good, and inherently free, but it was society that had a corrupting influence on them. Therefore, he suggests that the artificiality of formal schooling should not be introduced to youngsters until the age of 15. Prior to that age, through the guidance of a tutor, yet finding no need for books, children can learn through a developmental process that unfolds as a result of the children acting on their own impulses, interests, and curiosities, clearly underscoring the critical link between nature and experience and the inherent goodness of children (Crain, 2000; Ozmon & Craver, 1990).

The above suggests that Rousseau believed that from childhood to adulthood one progresses along in stages, underscoring the idea that growth is a developmental process that is intrinsically and biologically dictated. That is, according to the plan of nature (or a process of biological maturation), children, for the most part, grow and learn on their own as opposed to being taught by environmental influences, that is, what is taught by the teacher or any other external force. To that end, Rousseau saw the mind as a unique organism with its own innate patterns of thinking and acting, growing and learning, through experiences and interaction with the world. In a very real way, Rousseau promoted what is contemporarily referred to as a "child-centered" philosophy of education (Crain, 2000).

HORACE MANN (1796–1859)

With Horace Mann being at the forefront of leading the common school movement in the 1830s, he is considered the "father" of public education in the United States, and one who sought to make the Jeffersonian connection between education and democracy (Kincheloe, Slattery, & Steinberg, 2000). Remember that prior to the advent of the common schools, schools were not free; girls were often excluded; schools were not open for everyone; and attendance was not compulsory.

While in 1647 the "Old Deluder Satan" Act was passed,[3] whereby settlements with 50 families or more were required to assign a teacher to teach reading and writing, and for settlements of over a 100 families, a grammar school was required, the act was only lightly enforced and also insinuated that parents had to pay for school, conspicuously leaving it at the whim of parents whether their young ones would attend (Kaestle, 2008; Longstreet & Shane, 1993; Nauman, 2010; Ornstein & Hunkins, 2004).

Consequently, formal schooling ostensibly was reserved for a small minority, leaving many young people to work in the fields and learn literacy and life skills chiefly at home. Witnessing a growth in population after the Revolutionary War, an increase in poverty, and the simultaneous promotion of democratic principles, it became apparent that some kind of universal education system was a need (Kaestle, 2008).

Instituted in 1826 by law in Massachusetts, townships were expected to create school boards, which a little over a decade later prompted the establishment of the first state board of education in which Horace Mann was named commissioner. For Mann, with particular attention on the "three Rs," the idea for a "common school" was to create a system that was publically supported whereby opportunity for all children regardless of economic, social, religious, or political standing would harmoniously work together (Nauman, 2010; Ornstein & Hunkins, 2004).

In addition, Mann had established a teacher education program, the first of its kind in the growing nation. Particularly in light of an approach to teaching that was riddled with coercive practices—the approach of the day—Mann and other educational leaders looked to Europe for more appropriate ways that teachers could direct their practice. European educational leaders such as the Swiss Johann Heinrich Pestalozzi (1746–1827), with his emphasis that the teacher acts as a guide where students learn through experience; the German Friedrich Wilhelm Froebel (1782–1852), the "father" of kindergarten; and others argued for more of a child-centered approach whereby learning was an unfolding natural process that occurred through student interest, activity, and experience.

Finally, another German, Johann Friedrich Herbart (1776–1841) viewed the teaching and learning process not as a natural unfolding, as did Froebel, but rather as involving a systematic approach whereby teachers taught or built subjects upon one another (Longstreet & Shane, 1993).

In the final analysis, Mann saw a publically sponsored education system as one that would be the great equalizer in fostering the common good.

JOHN DEWEY (1859–1952)

The progressive education movement in the United States emerged out of the progressive reform era during the late 1800s and early 1900s. Grounded in the European thought of Rousseau, Pestalozzi, and Froebel, and later in the United States in the work of Francis W. Parker and others, John Dewey profoundly shaped the direction of the progressive education movement with his emphasis on pragmatism or experimentalism. Fundamental to the pragmatist is experience (Webb, Metha, & Jordan, 2007).

At a time when progressives thought that American schools were not serving students well with a top-down standardization model of education and a growing emphasis on the "science" of education, which, led by Edward L. Thorndike and others, focused on "precisely measuring" students, Dewey's voice was a breath of fresh air. To be sure, Dewey was an advocate of the science of education, but a social science, which interweaved psychology, philosophy, and sociology (Lagemann, 2000).

For Dewey and the progressive education movement, teaching is an endeavor in which the teacher thoughtfully considers the backgrounds of the children, their experiences, gifts, talents, and interests, in light of the teacher's knowledge of subject matter, methods, and students. In other words, Dewey cultivated the idea of the teacher as a professional who was empowered to "make teaching more individually responsive rather than more formulaic" (Darling-Hammond, 2006, p. 77).

To place his ideas in practice, Dewey founded the University Laboratory School at the University of Chicago in 1896 where the approach was child centered as opposed to subject centered. As the question goes, does a teacher teach a child or a subject matter? This is not a question of semantics, and Dewey, of course, would argue that teachers teach children. Through a process of facilitation, practices that are developmentally appropriate, and spaces that are democratically situated, children would experientially learn. Seeing the formal educational experience as a seamless extension to what all children individually bring from their home environment, Dewey saw education as "a process of living and not a preparation for future living" (Dewey, 1964, p. 430). In short, Dewey saw education as an endeavor to prepare youngsters to be active, engaged participants in a democratic society.

Dewey (1933) also importantly contributed to what it means to be a teacher, critically underscoring the importance of personal disposition and making clear that while one may possess methodological knowledge and even have desire, this attitudinal or dispositional state is not enough. What is also needed is an "understanding of the forms and techniques that are the channels through which these attitudes operate to the best advantage" (p. 30). In other words, for particular suitable dispositions to manifest themselves in practice, Dewey further suggests those dispositions must be cultivated through an attitude of open-mindedness (i.e., to consider multiple points of view and possibilities), whole-heartedness (i.e., an undivided heart in order to absorb what we learn; a genuine enthusiasm), and responsibility (i.e., taking into thoughtful consideration one's beliefs and the consequences of those beliefs; to responsibly engage students in meaningful subject matter).

The focused cultivation of these three attitudes are integral, leading to what Dewey describes as a "habit of thinking" influencing the formation of character (Dewey, 1933). The implication is that the routine of habit in the context of thinking implies that habits are not some mindless rulings that direct us; rather, thought informs our habits as a way of being, thinking, and doing (Dewey, 1983).

John Dewey's ideas were strongly influenced by other educators of his time, including several prominent women such as Ella Flagg Young, Jane Addams, and Lucy Sprague Mitchell, who are briefly discussed here.

ELLA FLAGG YOUNG (1845-1918)

While Dewey was at the University of Chicago, he consulted frequently with Ella Flagg Young who—with her experience with children and her practical experience as a school administrator and teacher—greatly informed him (Aldridge & Christensen, 2013). Aside from Dewey, Young also had her own ideas about education, which were richly expounded in *Isolation in the School* (Young, 1901). In short, she critically observed that "students and teachers alike increasingly had been stripped of their capacity to make meaningful decisions about their daily conditions or their assigned tasks" (Blount, 2002, p. 171). Therefore, one of Young's major contributions was her belief that teachers and students should be permitted more autonomy and decision making with regard to their learning. She was further able to expound this belief through her pioneering work as the first woman superintendent of the Chicago Schools and the first woman president of the National Education Association.

JANE ADDAMS (1860-1935)

Although often considered the most famous woman in the United States in the early 1990s and influential on John Dewey's thinking, Jane Addams is frequently neglected from the history of education because she saw education as encompassing much more than the classroom (Elshtain, 2002; Knight, 2010). In 1889 she opened the settlement house known as Hull House in Chicago, where over time it served as a comprehensive educational and social welfare facility center where a library was established, along with the offering of kindergarten classes, drama classes, a night school for adults, and finally, a boarding facility for women (Aldridge & Christensen, 2013).

Addams contributions to education emphasized not only the whole individual but also the person imbedded and interacting in multiple contexts, including social, economic, and political environments that must be incorporated for every person to have a comprehensive education. Her contributions to education and social welfare included her support for child labor laws, work to establish compulsory school attendance, her activism as a founding member of the American Civil Liberties Union, and her support and encouragement of other women educators such as the aforementioned Ella Flagg Young (Aldridge & Christensen, 2013).

LUCY SPRAGUE MITCHELL (1878–1967)

While John Dewey promoted progressive education, Lucy Sprague Mitchell was fully engaged in its practice. Mitchell founded the Bureau of Educational Experiments (BEE) in Greenwich Village (Mitchell, 1953), which eventually became the Bank Street College of Education and, located in New York City, continues to the present day as a major innovator in teacher education. Mitchell not only believed that teacher candidates should have direct and ongoing experience with children in classrooms but also was a pioneer in naturalistic observation and qualitative research in education (Antler, 1987). Indeed, her work with children helped inspire the developmentally appropriate practice guidelines of the National Association for the Education of Young Children (Copple & Bredekamp, 2009).

MARIA MONTESSORI (1870–1952)

Maria Montessori is well known for an approach to schooling that bears her name. As a young person aspiring to become a doctor and against tremendous gender discrimination, Montessori was among the first women who were awarded a medical degree in Italy. As a women's rights activist and an esteemed doctor who gravitated toward psychiatry, she demonstrated great compassion and care for her patients regardless of economic class or social class. This led her to a deep interest and study in education, with a particular focus on working with children with developmental delays who were thought to be uneducable. Based on her observations and how these children responded to simple activities such as threading beads and manipulating objects, Montessori came to realize that they were, in fact, capable of learning if the environmental conditions were developmentally and appropriately facilitated (Crain & Fite, 2013).

In its essence, a Montessori approach is one that is not moved by what children "should" learn; rather, the task of the teacher is to facilitate an environment in which children—who are natural learners or naturally curious—are provided choices to freely manipulate, discover, and explore through hands-on types of activities. This facilitated freedom is counter to a standardized environment that requires students to "perform" in which they are extrinsically awarded with such elements as grades, stickers, and the like. The artificiality of the latter actually robs children in many ways, including richly taking in the marvel of nature in all its forms, which deeply illuminates and reveals (Crain & Fite, 2013).

Built on the work of Rousseau, Pestalozzi, and Froebel that focuses on a child-centered approach to teaching and learning, Montessori schools have stood the test of time the world over.

THURGOOD MARSHALL (1908–1993)

With W. E. B. DuBois as one of its founding members, the National Association for the Advancement of Colored People (NAACP) was established in 1909 and has as its main goal to eradicate racism and prejudice and to promote political, economic, social, and educational equality for minorities. The NAACP served as an integral bridge to the modern-day civil rights movement, where determined activists for justice emerged, such as civil rights attorney Thurgood Marshall (NAACP, n.d.; Taylor, 1976).

Building on his prior civil rights work, Marshall went on to full-time work as legal counsel for the NAACP in 1936. And while he successfully argued several civil rights cases, it was the historical 1954 Supreme Court case *Brown v Topeka Board of Education* that thrust Marshall front and center as a civil rights icon. Taking on the Brown case, Marshall and his associates were arguing against a steep historical backdrop that in the 1890s saw southern states put into place literacy tests, poll taxes, and other mechanisms that hindered the possibility for Blacks to vote (Biography, 2014).[4]

And then it was the 1896 *Plessy v Ferguson Supreme Court* case that legitimized the "separate but equal" dogma, stamping an approval of the Jim Crow South with its sanctioning of separation and segregation, such as in schools, in theaters, at water fountains, in bathrooms, on buses and trains, and just about every other public space, even private facilities. Clearly Jim Crow alienated African Americans from educational equality and social and economic opportunities, and further exacerbated the emergence of a new wave of the KKK terror (Lewis & Lewis, 2009; Mann, 2007; Williams, 1987).

Filing on behalf of a group of Black parents who were forced to send their children to attend all-Black segregated schools in Topeka, Kansas, Marshall argued that the notion of "separate but equal" does not equate to equality in education; rather, educational facilities that are separate are inherently unequal, ultimately declaring that segregated public schools are in violation of the equal protection clause under the 14th Amendment. Particularly in the South, this ruling was received with great resistance. Therefore, the case was followed up with a Brown II ruling in 1955, instructing "with all deliberate speed" to terminate desegregation (Biography, 2014; Tiedt & Tiedt, 2005).

While it has been and still is a challenging task to integrate the nation's public schools, the Brown case was precedent-setting toward fostering a more integrated country. It was also during that time that Martin Luther King Jr. emerged on the public scene, along with Rosa Parks, Medgar Evers, Malcolm X, and a host of other civil rights activists, leading to other landmark changes such as the Voting Rights Act of 1965, which virtually destroyed the various mechanisms that kept African Americans from voting.

EXPANSION OF CIVIL RIGHTS IN EDUCATION

Off the heels of the powerful momentum that the civil rights movement generated in prompting awareness and activism, others looked to expand the idea of equity, equality, and justice in other areas in education. To simply name a few examples, consider the 1968 Bilingual Education Act (BEA), introduced by Ralph Yarborough (D-TX, 1957–1971). As a result of recognizing the specific needs of Spanish-speaking students from low-income households and limited English speaking proficiency, federal funds were allocated to school districts in order to provide bilingual education.

The BEA further prompted civil right workers to be active in expanding the meaning and intent of the act, particularly exemplified in the 1974 *Lau v Nichols* ruling, which stated that schools are required to provide supplemental language instruction for all non-English-speaking students. The Lau case favored Chinese students in the San Francisco area who were limited in educational opportunity because of their struggles with English. These cases and others paved the way to providing an equitable and just education for all, regardless of any types of possible language barriers.

To cite another example of expanding civil rights, and in response to students with disabilities who were denied or had limited access to public education, Public Law 94-142 was passed in the United States in 1975. Referred to as the Education for All Handicapped Children Act sponsored by Senator Harrison A. Williams Jr. (D-NJ, 1959–1982), this landmark legislation guaranteed a free and appropriate education for students with disabilities, in which the notion of individualized education programs (IEPs) and least restrictive environment entered in the education lexicon. To expand the meaning and intent of PL 94-142, further legislation was passed in subsequent years to better meet the appropriate needs for students with disabilities (e.g., see Public Laws 99-457, 101-476, 105-17, and 108-446).[5]

Finally, authored by Birch Bayh (D-IN, 1962–1981), the passing of the 1972 Title IX to the Higher Education Act was a momentous piece of legislation in which gender discrimination was declared illegal, opening doors for women to be more equally considered to enter law or medical school and other historically male-dominated programs. In addition, Title IX has also changed the face of women's athletics in terms of facilitating a more equitable funding formula for scholarships and facilities, which over the years has enabled an exponential rise in women participating in athletics on university campuses, and even at the high school level, across the United States.

THE ADVENT OF MULTICULTURAL EDUCATION

In addition to the above, emerging out of the civil rights movement, and also the women's rights movement, the work of James Banks, Christine Sleeter, and Sonia Nieto, among others, paved the way to placing multicultural education and culturally relevant teaching in its rightful place as an emphasis when it comes to the pedagogical process. A brief historical context may be helpful to better appreciate the urgent cry that prompted a turning point toward an education that works to unify in recognizing and celebrating our differences.

From the thinking and action that guided the Discovery Doctrine to the mindset of the early Puritans, the *Johnson v M'INtosh* Supreme Court case, and the idea of Manifest Destiny, the White Anglo-Saxon Protestant (WASP) ideal filtered through the branding of a newly formed United States. The WASP point of view controlled the economic, political, social, and religious establishment; hence the dominant culture in the United States set in motion an assimilationist ideology in which "being American and democratic was equated with conforming to the Anglo-Saxon pattern of language, morality, and behavior, and the immigrants were to give up their own cultural norms" (Pai & Adler, 2001, p. 60). Then came the need to recognize the importance of multicultural education, which has affected awareness among schoolchildren across the country.

And while the WASP tradition continues to influence our legal and political systems and how we operate institutions such as schools, banks, and government (Gollnick & Chinn, 2013), an overall mindset in that tradition has waned to a minority point of view, giving rise to the notion that there is strength and value in difference and diversity, and dismantling the myth of the "melting pot" concept. While the intent of this concept was to recognize ethnic and cultural differences in a dynamic that would harmoniously "melt" into a unique blend of what America is, what happened was "the brew turned out to be Anglo-Saxon again . . . reinforce[ing] the ethnocentrism of the majority and convince[ing] ethnic minorities that their ethnicity and cultural heritage were illegitimate and hence needed to be abandoned" (Pai & Adler, 2001, p. 63).

Therefore, the melting pot metaphor has been replaced by a more accurate one: the United States and its diverse makeup can instead be referred to as "tossed salad" (Tiedt & Tiedt, 2005). That is, while a certain amount of assimilation naturally occurs among diverse peoples into a unified whole, it is not at the expense of denying cultural, language, and ethnic traditions, which are all rooted in a pluralistic ideology. Moreover, it is also noteworthy to mention that the "tossed salad" metaphor implies that one ought not view diversity through a "colorblind" lens, which simply reinforces the dominant point of view and negates the variety in the salad, as it were, that is, the diversity that actually is.

In the end, what was started by the early forerunners of multicultural education, leading to the present day where a plethora of literature exists, well informs teacher education programs, teachers, and school districts all over the country. The work of diverse thinkers whose focus of interest or emphasis is varied—but in its totality embodies the complexity that is inherent when it comes to realizing and honoring the pluralistic society the United States actually is—and suggests there is no formula or one right way to teach a diverse student population.

ETHNIC STUDIES AND ABORIGINAL/ INDIGENOUS STUDIES PROGRAMS

Near simultaneously during the emergence of multicultural education, activists, largely led by students of color, challenged university systems that lacked substantive numbers of professors of color, that predominately focused on a Eurocentric curriculum, and that imposed inadequate measures regarding access to higher education for minority groups. Particularly from the activism that first evolved from California, ethnic studies programs and departments began to be a part of the curriculum in universities, spreading across the country. In brief, while the emphasis of respective programs may vary from setting to setting, central to ethnic studies' programs is critically examining the role of race, ethnicity, and the reexamination and reconstruction of history that has been historically neglected (Hu-DeHart, 1993).

In addition to the development of ethnic studies programs in universities across the United States, aboriginal and indigenous studies programs have also become particularly prevalent in Canada, Australia, Latin America, and other places. Certainly varying from respective university settings, these programs look to critically deconstruct the lens of colonial rule and deeply examine the place of indigenous language, culture, values, heritages, and legacies.

PAULO FREIRE (1921–1997)

Considered by many to be the "father" of critical pedagogy, Paulo Freire is most known for his landmark book *Pedagogy of the Oppressed*, which was originally published in 1968.

Based on his experiences and observations in his native Brazil and exilic period in Chile, the text explores multiple themes related to the exploitive nature of political, social, religious, and educational systems that summarily marginalize groups of people. In addition to "denouncing" oppressive structures, Freire simultaneously "announces" ways in which the oppressed can be moved to a place of critical consciousness through processes that promote a democratizing climate. In sum—although not withstanding his numerous later brilliant works—*Pedagogy* is perhaps the best and most concise presentation of the critical aspects of Freire's philosophy, particularly relative to his making the distinction between the concept of a banking approach to education and a problem-posing approach, and between the notion of humanization and dehumanization (Roberts, 2000).

The antithesis of a banking approach to education (devoid of the learner's cultural-socio-historical reality and antidialogically driven) is what Freire characterizes as a problem-posing education. In this approach, the driving assumptions are that people are viewed as conscious beings who are unfinished and yet are in the process of becoming; liberation occurs through cognitive acts as opposed to the transfer of information (Freire, 1990). A problem-posing approach unfolds in a dialogical setting, which is not to say that dialogue is simply a "conversation" or a mere sharing of ideas. Moreover, in a Freirean sense, dialogue is more than the Socratic concept when Socrates uses it as a teaching tool in order for subjects to rediscover forgotten ideas or knowledge (Collins, 1977; Freire, 1985).

Rather, embedded in the element of dialogue is criticality in problematizing the existential reality of the subject, a process in which students are presented with problems relative to their relationship with the world, leading them to be challenged yet prompted to respond to that challenge within a context of other interrelated problems (Freire, 1990, 1985). In that light, therefore, authentic dialogue fosters a horizontal relationship between educator and learner that affects building trust whereby the dialogical occurrence begins with the learners as the subjects engaged in a process whereby they play an integral role as creators and makers of their world (Freire, 1985; Freire, 1994).

Finally, dialogue and the notion of praxis (the dialectical interweaving of theory and practice) cultivates Freire's concept of *conscientização* (conscientization), which is an unfolding process that is filtered through a contextual framework that intersects the psychological-political-theological-social milieu in the awakening of critical awareness (Freire, 1994). The idea of conscientization is not static or formulaic but rather situated in historical spaces and times, implying that the process is not a blueprint to indicate how it unfolds for every individual regardless of their society, location, and era (Freire, 1994; Roberts, 2000).

ACTIVISM MATTERS

Along with the several others that were given a nod in this narrative, the work of Socrates, Rousseau, Mann, Dewey, Montessori, Marshall, Young, Addams, Mitchell, and Freire is critically significant as each in their own way, in their unique circumstances, and in the time frame they found themselves were compelled to respond to a misdirected, faulty, or unjust practice or policy. Their active commitment to some kind of change triggered a turning point in historically and influentially shaping the trajectory of education with respect to policy, pedagogical practice, and curricula considerations.

Socrates, in response to a formal didactic way of working with students, taught us to question, to look within to reason, and to critically think through certain realities in some shape or form. Significantly informing pedagogical practice, the idea of a Socratic approach to teaching is common parlance for those in education. Rousseau, instead of viewing a child as a "blank slate" and emphasizing that children learn differently than adults, is considered an important framer of what we know today as developmentally appropriate practice, certainly influencing the work of Jean Piaget, Maria Montessori, and others.

Arguably the most influential educators in American history are Horace Mann and John Dewey. Mann, in response to a clear lack of educational opportunity during the early formation of the United States, saw a need for a system of education that was open to the public; hence public education was born. And Dewey, with the critical contribution of such people as Ella Flagg Young, Jane Addams, and Lucy Sprague Mitchell, responded to an often-disconnected didactic approach to teaching and learning in favor of meaningfully connecting theory to practice, with an emphasis on education that is experiential and democratic in nature—striking at the foundational heart of the progressive movement in the United States and beyond.

With a deep care for the disabled, the poor, and the rights of women, Maria Montessori's work was a clear and present response to educational malpractice; her work has had a sustaining worldwide impact to this day. And

Thurgood Marshall leads the list of anyone in working toward furthering civil rights in education policy in the United States, blowing the doors wide open to redefining and expanding the meaning and intent of civil rights and ushering in the importance of a culturally relevant approach to pedagogical practice. Finally, Paulo Freire crystallizes for us that education is a political enterprise, that standing on the sidelines is not an option, and that to plead neutrality when it comes to decisions relative to practices and policies is not a choice.

In the final analysis, all of these individuals were immersed in the community and tapped into an activism spirit, resulting in constructively turning the trajectory of education. We have learned much from these forerunners. This begs the following question: what is currently happening in education that demands us to move toward an activist turning-point response? In part 2, we examine the external forces that systematically work to deprofessionalize what it means to be a teacher, to dismantle public education, and to undermine traditional teacher education programs.

Second, as will be discussed in part 3, we consider the internal forces that teacher education as a whole must question, contend, resolve, and then come to terms with at respective institutional sites.

Indeed, whether from external or internal forces affecting teacher education, an activist turning-point response is in order.

NOTES

1. We have intentionally placed here an emphasis on individuals who have worked to constructively make the world a more just and qualitatively better place to live. Obviously, throughout history there have been miscreants of all stripes who have also changed the course of history with their destructive conduct.

2. Although John Locke (1632–1704) is widely known for his significant contribution in shaping the founding documents of the United States, he has also been an important voice in shaping the direction of developmental psychology. Most famously, Locke proposed that a newborn's mind is a "white paper, void of all characters, without any ideas" (Locke, 1690, bk. 2, chap. 1, sec. 2). In other words, the infant's mind is a tabula rasa (blank slate), meaning it is through experience with the outside environment that one comes to know. The idea that one learns or comes to know through experience is rooted in the idea of Francis Bacon's concept of empiricism. While Locke's idea of the mind being a blank slate may have its place, it does has its limitations or shortcomings in that this viewpoint sees the mind as too passively dependent on external forces, meaning the mind itself is not an active, innate agent in the formulation of thought. Despite the critical observation of the latter, for Locke, education is ultimately a process of becoming more fully human (Crain, 2000; Ozmon & Craver, 1990).

3. The act implied that learning to read armed one to avoid Satan's deception of keeping one from reading the scriptures by remaining illiterate.

4. It is important to note that Mamie Phipps Clark (1917–1983) initiated the foundational research contributing to the Brown case (Aldridge & Christensen, 2013). In fact, it was Clark, along with her husband, who was at the forefront to study identity in African American children (ages 3–7), which led to the illuminating "doll test" (Guthrie, 1990). In their study, Clark found "over one-half of the children preferred a white doll or rejected the brown doll" (Guthrie, 1990, p. 68). This research, therefore, was used as evidence in the Brown case that separate was not equal. In many cases, segregated African American children tended to see themselves as inferior, leading Clark to argue that segregation influenced the way children construct race and their identity (Clark, 1983).

5. To be sure, the civil rights movement, and legal decisions such as *Brown vs. Topeka Board of Education*, helped open the door for educational initiatives for students with disabilities, even though the history of special education can be traced back several centuries. And while special education has had numerous successes during the past 100 years, it still has a long way to go. The development of socially constructed labels for children with disabilities, the disproportionate number of certain populations in special education, and the need for more inclusive programs involving interdisciplinary practices remain concerning. That is, there are still disproportionate numbers of minorities in special education classes. Children and adolescents of color are overrepresented in classes for the disabled and underrepresented in programs for the gifted (Black, 2010).

II
THE HIJACKING OF THE EDUCATION NARRATIVE

• 2 •

Reform, Accountability, and Compromising K–12 Education

For the last 40 years, if there is one concept that is at the top of the list as a subject of conversation on education, that concept is reform. And a close second, which is intimately attached to reform, is the notion of accountability. They are really two pleasing concepts in their raw meaning. For example, consider the words *improvement*, *reorganization*, and *restructuring* as synonyms for reform, and think about the words *responsibility*, *answerability*, and *bond* as similar to the concept of accountability. From a structural level, a system level, and even a personal level, the idea of a discussion about reform and accountability implores the idea of moving forward and growth. That is a good thing.

Yet today, when those two concepts are raised in the context of pre-K–12 education, their meanings have been narrowly reduced to centrally mean that the actions of school reform unfold as teachers are held accountable for ensuring that students do well on high-stakes tests. Incentivized by monetary and other extrinsic awards in a competitive schooling climate, the assumption is that when the students *perform* well on such tests, reform is taking place and teacher accountability is working (Kirylo & Nauman, 2006).

Conversely, if students *perform* poorly, teachers are the blame, and students are placed in various types of remedial stations, indicative of accountability in action as well. This imposed climate of reform and accountability reaches its climax in the shutdown of schools and the facilitation of opening charter schools, the promotion of vouchers, and the ushering in of fast-track types of teacher preparation programs.

In that light, the assumption that drives reform and the need for accountability is that our schools are broken and need to be fixed, and to fix broken schools, a heavy-handed top-down lever will be levied. And the steering of that lever is to be driven by an environment that is competitively driven. In other words, as in a capitalistic-driven society, where profit is the goal, businesses of whatever type compete for the best brand and the most sales. The idea of a free market economy impels the work and effort, meaning that "a rising tide lifts all boats" (i.e., the product). Or if you prefer, take a sporting analogy to explain a competitively driven reform and accountability model, whereby through competition the "survival of the fittest" will rise to the top and take first place, yet will presumably "force" all other competitors to work hard to reach that pinnacle too.

Not only does this competitive model currently permeate pre-K–12 education, but also it has forced teacher education programs to examine their role in preparing teacher candidates, a multilayered challenge that will later be discussed. But for now, we must first contextually examine how we got to this place where the idea of educating our youth has been hijacked by a narrative that is now near-exclusively filtered by a parlance of business and competition as opposed to an endeavor that continuously seeks to improve in engaging our youth in rich, meaningful learning environments.

NOT AN OVERNIGHT HAPPENING

The reductionist explanation of what contemporary education has become has been a gradual, nearly 40-year process, beginning with the 1983 *Nation at Risk* report released under the Reagan administration.[1] A defined shift in how public education and teachers were viewed began to take place in which the report declared that test scores were declining, the curriculum was outdated, and the quality of teaching had gone down, all of which contributed to the "rising tide of mediocrity," greatly placing the economic and national security of the nation at risk (U.S. National Commission on Excellence in Education, 1983). Improving the curriculum in the schools, working on strengthening teacher education programs, and the adoption of more rigorous measurable standards for both K–12 and university programs was in order.

Of course, *A Nation at Risk* was a highly charged document, largely placing the presumed failure of education at the feet of educators and public education. The report, however, did not go unchallenged, particularly underscored in the still-popular book titled *The Manufactured Crises* (1995) by David Berliner and Bruce Biddle, who eloquently questioned the assumptions and data that propelled the publication of the *Nation at Risk* report, concluding that the quality of schools are not failing as purported; rather, the larger problem confronting schools are economic, societal, and poverty issues.

Nevertheless, *A Nation at Risk* gained traction and was foundational in influencing the direction of subsequent reform initiatives such as America 2000 (G. H. W. Bush), Goals 2000 (Clinton), the No Child Left Behind Act (NCLB; G. W. Bush), Race to the Top program (Obama), and the Trump administration's education policies. As one examines each of these reform packages, it becomes apparent that the emphasis on assessment increasingly rises in importance. And with NCLB, the culmination of that importance takes center stage, attaching "high stakes" to testing.[2]

Moreover, notably commenced under the George W. Bush administration, we see how then secretary of education Rodney Paige touted "highly qualified" teachers yet simultaneously besmirched traditional teacher education programs and showed favor for fast-track preparation programs. The propping up of fast-track teacher preparation programs gave fuel to the legitimization of such organizations as Teach for America (TFA) and other types of fast-tracked-related nonprofit and for-profit programs.

In short, TFA, with its Peace Corps–type mission, is a program where college graduates in whatever discipline receive several weeks of "teacher training" and are then released to teach in mostly high-poverty schools. Perhaps it can go without being said, but placing TFA teachers in high-poverty schools means assigning the most underqualified and least experienced teachers to these schools. Yet in the higher economic level areas where academic achievement is high, teachers are required to possess a degree from a reputable university teacher education program and to be certified, and in many instances, a master's degree is assumed (Fischetti & Kirylo, 2015).

One can only conclude, therefore, the expectations for what it takes to be a teacher, what it means to be a teacher, and the professionalism involved is weighted more heavily for some schools than for others. Yet, as John Dewey (1943) gently chides, "what the best and wisest parent wants for his own child, that must the community want for all of its children. Any other ideal for our schools is narrow and unlovely; acted upon, it destroys our democracy" (pp. 6–7).

Thus, taking this cue from Dewey, why then are the expectations for teacher qualifications in higher economic districts not the same where the poverty rate is high? Would the parents in higher economic level districts be accepting of underqualified teachers teaching their children? Of course not. Then why are we not outraged by the infrastructure that touts underqualified teachers for the poor?

The indictment here is not on what may be the good intent of some of the individuals who make the two-year commitment to teach under the umbrella of TFA; rather, the condemnation is on the calculated infrastructure that aggressively promotes such organizations. Not only does advancing programs such as Teach for America, Teach for All, the New Teacher Project,

Teachers of Tomorrow, and Academic Pathway to Teaching, to name a few, foster the deprofessionalization of what it means to be a teacher,[3] but also this deprofessionalization has spilled over into the administrative ranks, to the highest levels.

To illustrate the point, consider the rise of John White, superintendent of education for the State of Louisiana. White, a TFA alum, with no degree in education, taught for a mere three years (1999–2002), but apparently enough to thrust him into the role as executive director for TFA, Chicago, and for TFA, New Jersey. Later, he worked under Mayor Michael Bloomberg and Chancellor Joe Klein as deputy chancellor in New York. In 2011, White then caught the attention of Paul Pastorek, albeit a noneducator, yet superintendent of education for the State of Louisiana.

An attorney and one who pounced on a post-Katrina recovery agenda that paved down the road of privatization, Pastorek announced that White would be appointed as the new superintendent for the Recovery School District (RSD) (Louisiana Department of Education, 2011), despite never being an assistant principal or a principal and without required certification. No matter, after serving in the role as the RSD superintendent only a short eight months, White was elevated to the role of superintendent of education for the State of Louisiana in January 2012, obviously Pastorek's ultimate motive on who he wanted as his replacement.

It is worth noting, though troublingly, that during the time frame under White's administration, Chas Roemer was president of the Louisiana Board of Elementary and Secondary Education (BESE) who suggested that an undergraduate degree is not necessarily a prerequisite to be a teacher. As if that were not enough to raise eyebrows, in bewildering terms at a local school board meeting in Tangipahoa Parish, Louisiana, White asserted that he was not "keen" on teacher certification, making the point that all that is necessary to teach is a college degree and that one simply be proficient (Fischetti & Kirylo, 2015; Ravitch, 2012b).

In that light, it should be no surprise that TFA tripled its post-Katrina presence in Louisiana, and that many alumni are now serving as principals, advocates, and CEOs within the state K–12 education structure (Sondel, 2013).[4] In the final analysis, Louisiana is but one example that demonstrates the erosion of the professionalism of what is required and what it takes to be an educator. But there is precedent here.

Take the case of Margaret Spellings, the secretary of education who followed Rodney Paige, under the George W. Bush administration. At her confirmation hearing, Spellings claimed that she has "seen education from many angles" (Robelen, 2005, p. 3). Of course, she had been involved in government work as a policy maker, but she, as in the case of Pastorek, has never "seen" education as a student teacher, paraprofessional, teacher, assistant principal, principal, school guidance counselor, itinerant social worker, school psychologist, central office administrator, superintendent, or education professor. Moreover, she did not hold a graduate degree, and her undergraduate degree is in political science.

So, what was it about Spellings that made her "highly qualified" to be appointed to one of the most visible education positions in the land? According to G. W. Bush, she was qualified because he worked with Spellings for more than a decade and had come to rely "on her intellect and judgment" (Robelen, 2005, p. 2).[5] Providing props to the appointment of Spellings, University of Denver adjunct education professor Carol Kelly curiously put it this way: "I don't believe that lack of an advanced degree or experience as an educator should disqualify her from serving as U.S. secretary of education" (Robelen, 2005, p. 2).[6] One can only imagine the pushback if applying Kelly's line of thinking for a surgeon general appointment.

Then there was the appointment of Michelle Rhee, another TFA alum, who was thrust into the new created chancellor position of the Washington, D.C., schools in 2007, answering to the mayor. Dictatorial and overconfident, self-assured in her leadership approach, Rhee went on a "firing" campaign, letting scores of teachers go because of low test scores; yet in 2010, she left her post in disgrace, dogged by a test-cheating scandal scheme. No problem. Rhee's name emerged in consideration for secretary of education for the Trump administration. That position, however, fell in the lap of Betsy DeVos, a billionaire heiress from Michigan who was, again, a noneducator, but one with a history to destroy Horace Mann's idea of education for the common good, that is, dismantling public education.

DeVos's confirmation came with great controversy, as she demonstrated a woeful lack of understanding educational public policy and the multiple facets of curriculum and pedagogy, notwithstanding that she thinks, "government really sucks."[7] Yet, a short few months after her confirmation, she is using "government power to change policy toward her liking, which has largely been to dismantle what many saw as consumer and civil rights protections. . . . She is a prime example of the Trump model of government service: To use the power of the federal government with the stated purpose of returning power to states and localities but with the effect of directing policy toward her own policy goals."[8]

NOTES

1. In addition, it must be noted that the launch of Sputnik by the Soviet Union in 1957 placed them ahead of the United States in the space race, which sparked U.S. schools to reevaluate, in particular, the quality and effectiveness of science and mathematics education.

2. While Clinton's Goals 2000: Educate America Act *recommended* testing for grades 4, 8, and 12 to ascertain whether standards were being realized, in George W. Bush's NCLB Act, testing was *mandatory* in those grades. The stakes were certainly higher under NCLB, tied to "grade retention, admittance into special programs, graduation, admission into college, and whether or not schools remain open and teachers get to keep their jobs" (Solley, 2007, p. 33). It is also worth pointing out that in countries like the United Kingdom, Australia, and New Zealand, similar reforms have been undertaken. Standards and assessments were developed toward fostering a competitive, test-centric environment, along with punitive teacher evaluation systems. This has led to a market-driven schooling environment, opening the door to the notion of choice and charters, and further widening the gap between majority economically wealthy student populations and those who are without (Fischetti, 2018; Kirylo a, b, 2016).

3. Moreover, because of the itinerant nature of TFA where the "temp" comes in and stays a minimum of two years in a school community, often moving on elsewhere or getting out of education, a detrimental consequence is the creation of a "revolving door" of teachers in and out of a school community, which does no good to build relationships and the overall continuity of a school community.

4. For more detail on post-Katrina K–12 education in Louisiana, see Fischetti & Kirylo (2015).

5. Spellings was an education aide for the then governor Bush in Texas and is a principal architect of NCLB.

6. Again, recall, under the NCLB Act, a big emphasis was having "highly qualified" teachers in the classroom. Yet with what was obviously a lack of qualifications for the position of secretary of education, interestingly, Spellings was given a pass, was made an exception, and was not expected to jump through any of the NCLB standardization hoops. The justifications made for her appointment as secretary of education certainly had an undermining effect on teacher morale and what NCLB purported to support (in this case, as it relates to the highly qualified educator). One cannot expect an individual to take seriously a mandate when it is simply not respected at all levels. As Senator Birch Bayh of Indiana states in James Noll's (2004) book *Taking Sides: Clashing Views on Controversial Educational Issues*, "Everyone is for accountability until it actually gets put into place and applies to him" (p. 139).

7. See Strauss (2016).

8. See Strauss (2017).

• 3 •

Neoliberalism

A Systematic Effort to Privatize

Whether it is Paul Pastorek, John White, Margaret Spellings, Michelle Rhee, or Betsy DeVos, to highlight only a few, the common thread through all of them is that they are either "fast-tracked" noncertified educators or noneducators who all look to privatization as the route to "reform" education.

To walk that route, as it was jump-started by *A Nation of Risk*, they have to systematically and collectively blame public education and public school teachers for what specifically ails education, and generally ails society, ultimately providing the fuel for DeVos to declare that traditional public education has come to a "dead end."[1] Hence, the solution is to privatize.

The thinking that drives the trajectory toward privatization is rooted in neoliberal thought that is often linked to globalization, possessing an ideology that is market driven, promoting individualism, competition, and profit. In brief, the notion of neoliberalism emerged from the liberalism of the 1800s and beyond, which, in contrast to totalitarian regimes, politically looked to the market to dictate economic and social realities via a competitive enterprise in which freedom and liberation can be achieved. The latter is notwithstanding that in the United States there was still the furthering of such programs as Franklin D. Roosevelt's 1930s New Deal, Lyndon B. Johnson's 1960s Great Society ("war" on poverty and injustice), and more openness to the rights of workers and union formations.

However, when the Reagan administration came into power (1981–1989) with its release of *A Nation at Risk*, the administration also looked to weakened government social programs and unions (as demonstrated in the case of the Professional Air Traffic Controllers Organization) and fostered a story line that blamed the poor for living as "welfare queens" who were content living off the government.

Thus, during the 1980s, along with the support of Margaret Thatcher, the Reagan administration surfaced a new liberalism (i.e., neoliberalism) in which the injection of competition, deregulation, and a reliance on the force of the market is what steers societal and economic change. Monbiot (2016) explains it this way:

> Neoliberalism sees competition as the defining characteristic of human relations. It redefines citizens as consumers, whose democratic choices are best exercised by buying and selling, a process that rewards merit and punishes inefficiency. It maintains that "the market" delivers benefits that could never be achieved by planning. Attempts to limit competition are treated as inimical to liberty. Tax and regulation should be minimized, public services should be privatized. The organization of labour and collective bargaining by trade unions are portrayed as market distortions that impede the formation of a natural hierarchy of winners and losers. Inequality is recast as virtuous: a reward for utility and a generator of wealth, which trickles down to enrich everyone. Efforts to create a more equal society are both counterproductive and morally corrosive. The market ensures that everyone gets what they deserve. (para. 4, 5)

Indeed, neoliberalism is not only a system of economics but also a sociological viewpoint and a philosophy of life on how people ought to act.

And if they do not act a certain way, as dictated by that viewpoint, then the problem is them and not the viewpoint that created the conditions of their problem. In other words, for neoliberal thought to function, it has to have a scapegoat to advance its agenda. For Reagan and company—and up to this present day—it is the "welfare queens" who are the cause of their poverty because they are not working hard enough, having gotten comfortable living "off" the government.

Moreover, public education is doing poorly because teachers are not doing a good job, have become complacent, and are protected by tenure, and because unions keep in place such a system. Finally, the economy is not thriving and the middle class is shrinking because the burden of taxes is too high, regulation is too controlling, and government involvement stifles, suffocating the movement of the market.

The solution for the poor, the elixir for reforming education, and the way to grow the middle class is to get government out of the way, reduce taxes and government spending (including reducing housing assistance, lunch programs, and other social programs), deregulate, insert competition, and let the market forces drive the economic and social engine. By doing this, the presumption is that dollars are freed up, placed back (trickled down) into the hands of the people, which will open doors toward opportunity, the creation of jobs, and the making of choices. For example, to make the point in an education context, consider how reform currently functions in a test-centric environment.

Schools have become testing centers instead of learning centers, where students are competing among themselves; teachers are competing against other teachers; classrooms are competing against other classrooms; and schools, districts, and states are competing against each other. Students, teachers, and administrators—indeed entire schools—fall and rise on what these scores reveal. More graphically, as Alfie Kohn (2000) puts it, "standardized testing has swelled and mutated, like a creature in one of those old horror movies, to the point that it now threatens to swallow our schools whole" (p. 1).

And it is from this competition and the revelation of these scores that school-aged children are judged; that entire school communities are viewed; that teachers' jobs are at stake; that schools are closed; that the housing market is affected; that school choice, vouchers, and charter schools are advanced; and that alternative teacher certification programs and fast-tracked teacher preparation avenues are promoted, while working to take over traditional models of teacher education programs (more on this later). In short, corporate reformers, backed by deep pockets, have successfully manipulated the meaning and intent of assessment, using it for their own purposes.

Thus, where test scores are low, which are generally in high-poverty areas, the problem of low scores and poverty is not the social and economic conditions that cultivate poverty and the impact that poverty has on school readiness and learning; rather, the problem is the teachers and public education that are not doing a good job.

Therefore, the threat to close neighborhood schools is a solution, along with providing vouchers and opening for-profit and nonprofit charter schools. To do this, dollars must be sucked out of the public coffers in order to support the corporate reformers' entrepreneurial education venture, which has as its ultimate goal to dismantle public education, because after all it is "dead."

In the end, as Chomsky (2017) summarizes the meaning, "the simplest definition of 'neoliberalism' is 'let the market run everything.' Get the government out of policy formation except to support market activities" (p. 88). From the individual student taking a standardized test to the parents who feed their child a good breakfast on the day of the test so the child will do well; the public education teacher who teaches to the test; the school principal who blows the bugle of the high stakes of the test; and the corporate reformer who works to close a school contingent on the score of the test, competition lies at the heart of market activities, even at a school setting. And in a competition, there will always be winners and losers.

For the former, the winner will always favor the top 1 percent of the population (i.e., mega-corporate owners and the very rich) who can powerfully work—with their bags of cash—to get government out of policy formation in order to dictate the sway of the market, among other entities, regarding trade, health care, ecosystems, transportation, prisons, and education. And for the latter, the loser will be the public square and democratic spaces, most affecting the poor and marginalized.

Indeed, the workings toward dismissing public anything and union formation/collective bargaining, and dispersing demonstrations/protests, undermine solidarity and the power of the collective, as corporate reformers would like in order to maintain power. In other words, by maintaining the narrative of an Americana that props up the myth of the "rugged" individual (e.g., the "Marlboro Man" comes to mind[2]) will, ironically, only be cunningly manipulated by the collective influence of the rarified air of the individual nature of the top 1 percent as they see necessary.[3] It is no coincidence that a billionaire was confirmed secretary of education.

NOTES

1. See Strauss (2017).
2. Recall the "Marlboro Man" cigarette commercial from the 1950s to the 1990s, which worked to reflect strength and the "rugged" individual.
3. Chomsky (2017) further explains: "In a democracy, public opinion is going to have some influence on policy, and then the government carries out actions determined by the population. That's what democracy means. It is important to understand that privileged and powerful sectors have never liked democracy and for very good reasons. Democracy puts power into the hands of the general population and takes it away from the privileged and the powerful. It's a principle of concentration of wealth and power" (p. xiii). "In order to maintain that concentration of wealth and power, solidarity (i.e., the power of the people) needs to be attacked, dispersed, replaced by the individualism that says, 'You've got to be for yourself and follow the vile maxim—"don't care about others"'—which is okay for the rich and powerful, but devastating for everyone else. . . . We see it in the attack on public schools. Public schools are based on the principle of solidarity [as in the case of social security]. I no longer have children in school. They've grown up, but the principle of solidarity says, 'I happily pay taxes so that the kid across the street can go to school.' Now, that's normal human emotion. You have to *drive that out* of people's heads. 'I don't have kids in school. Why should I pay taxes? Privatize it,' and so on" (pp. 65–66).

· 4 ·

Working to Eliminate Traditional Teacher Education Programs

𝓘t is no secret that corporate reformers have teacher education on their radar. Following the testing regime script—as the thinking goes—if K–12 students are not doing well, it is the teacher's fault, and if it is the teacher's fault, by extension, it is the fault of the teacher education preparation program where that teacher received education. The latter, coupled with a teacher shortage and the fact that teacher education in and of itself has historically been swimming upstream in an ongoing struggle to gain respect, cooperate reformers have swooped in.

It must be noted, acutely magnified by No Child Left Behind (NCLB) and beyond, the loss of voice and autonomy, poor working conditions, the hyperfocus on a test-centric environment, and low pay has had a significant impact on the teacher shortage.[1] In general, approximately 20 percent of new teacher hires leave the profession within three years; moreover, approximately 50 percent of teachers working in urban areas leave the profession within five years.[2]

With respect to low pay, for example, consider several counties in South Carolina where the starting salary is $29,900. However, as of this writing, there seems to be a push to move that starting amount to $32,000, which will simply mean that the mere $2,100 increase will move a household of four from a threshold of $5,300 above the poverty line to $7,400 above that line.[3] More recently, however, the South Carolina state legislature agreed to give teachers a raise, albeit amounting to a paltry, if not insulting, 1 percent increase (Schechter, 2018).[4]

With that financial prospect and in light of having to pay off loans, added to the other factors mentioned above, many potential teacher candidates—who calculate these realities and those teachers who are living those realities (often working second jobs)—make the decision to either not enter the profession or leave after only a few short years in the field. In the end, it is clear that the state of education—from K–12 education to teacher education—is ripe for corporate reformers to systematically take over.

In higher education in general, this takeover works to weaken tenure, undermine academic freedom, and reduce the voice of faculty governance, all exacerbated with the increasing influx of itinerant adjuncts and instructors, and the overall defunding of higher education. In other words, the push is to turn faculties "into a labor force that mimics Walmart workers while the managerial class is expanding, draining off funds from faculty and students, and governing the university as if it were a branch of General Motors and Disneyland" (Harper, 2014, para. 8). Teacher education in specific is an exemplification of the managerial class expanding in order to turn teacher educators into "workers," as will be discussed shortly.

But first, Teach for America (TFA), with its built-in "worker" model structure, trains its membership with a test-centric model of schooling in mind. And whether it is at the national, state, school, or classroom level, TFA and other related types of fast-tracked teacher preparation programs have become "embedded" in school districts across the country with the assistance of stated-supported funding.

Legitimizing such programs with state dollars not only pulls money away from building the authentic professionalization of teacher education but also adds to the self-serving confidence level of the managerial class of the National Council on Teacher Quality (NCTQ) mentioned in the introduction of this text. If one simply takes a cursory examination of the individuals who lead and work for NCTQ and the governing board they answer to, it will be evident that they are made from the same corporatized cloth as John White, Betsy DeVos, and others. In sum, as Mike Rose asserts, "there is no need to speculate about the stance of Kate Walsh, the president of the National Council on Teacher Quality, for since her days as a senior policy analyst at the Abell Foundation in Baltimore, she has been a fierce critic of teacher education and an advocate for alternative credentialing programs" (Strauss, 2014, para. 19).[5]

Now, it seems many traditional teacher education programs around the country have been disturbingly seduced into looking toward the managerial class and worker paradigm as well. Think about Bill Gates who not only has worked hard in an attempt to shape K–12 education in a privatized image but also is focused on reforming teacher education in that image. For example, in 2016 the Gates Foundation awarded $35 million to a project called Teacher Preparation Transformation Centers funneled through five different projects, one of which is the Texas Tech–based University-School Partnerships for the Renewal of Educator Preparation (U.S. Prep) National Center.[6]

This Gates Foundation–backed project involves five teacher education programs in the country (Southern Methodist University, University of Houston, Jackson State University, University of Memphis, and Southeastern Louisiana University).[7] And the framework that guides this "renewal" of educator preparation comes from the National Institute for Excellence in Teaching (NIET), along with the peddling of their programs, the System for Teacher and Student Advancement (TAP) and the Student and Best Practices Center (BPC). Yet again, coming from another guy with bags of money, leading the charge of NIET is Lowell Milken (brother of junk bond king Michael Milken) who is chairman and TAP founder.[8]

In other words, in each respective college of education involved in the grant, despite the rich collective background of K–12 teaching experience, decades of teacher education work, a wealth of postgraduate education degrees, and involvement in educational research, the workers (i.e., education professors) were placed under obligation to be "trained" by the managerial class (i.e., NIET "certified" trainers).

With the acronym NIET inscribed on just about every page of presentation material, capped with an accompanying dense, bounded training manual titled *NIET Higher Education Handbook*, NIET trainers are self-assured of their "prescription" of success, which includes incorporating a slick, commercialized NIET website that leads to a labyrinth of materials, portals, aids, and how, when, and where a teacher educator must be *certified* in its brand.[9]

In the end, Wegwert and Foley (2017) are correct when they suggest that colleges of education are "fertile ground for the nurturance and protection of the artifacts and effects of neoliberal rationality: the erosion of democratic values and sensibilities and the reification of anti-intellectualism" (p. 55). In that light, therefore, there are two fundamental reasons teacher educators in particular must resist such programs as NIET.

First, the notion of being "trained" by such programs is being propelled by the similar story line that is at work to dismantle K–12 education. That is, for K–12 education, teachers have been blamed for all that ails society. From that position of blame, corporate reformers lunge with their obsessed focus on ratings, scoring, standardization, competition, and privatization. Similarly, as for teacher education programs, they are under attack with the same blame game for their supposed subpar operation, paving the way for a corporate takeover. Then comes the *NIET Higher Education Handbook* and NIET's purported claim of their proven comprehensive educator model to restructure and revitalize the teaching profession.[10] Clearly, the proverbial door is open to dismantle the relevance of teacher education programs.[11]

Second, if enough money is thrown their way, it appears that teacher education programs can be bought. Indeed, money is power; money is influence; and money shapes direction.[12] This is no truer than the dough that the Gates Foundation is doling out in its attempt to re-create teacher education in a corporatized image.

When teacher education programs become the petri dish to cultivate this image, the trajectory, again, not only works to undermine academic freedom, tenure, and the professorate, but also disturbingly contributes to their very nonrelevance as teacher education programs. They become centers for teacher training. While there is a certain interfacing between receiving training and receiving an education, those two paradigms of thought and practice serve two different purposes.

To draw from *Merriam-Webster* (2012), the notion of receiving training implies one learns the necessary skills to do a job or perform a craft, and the concept of receiving an education implies formal schooling at such places as a university. In other words, training suggests learning methods, techniques, and skills, simply steering prospective teachers to become functionaries or what Stokes (1997) describes as technicians who uncritically abide by a standardized or a one-size-fits-all model of doing things.

Indeed, as Freire (1998) rightly reminds us, the idea of teacher preparation being reduced to a form of training should never happen but rather should go beyond technical preparation, which is mindfully pervasive with criticality, igniting epistemological curiosity and is "rooted in the ethical formation both of selves and of history" (p. 23).

HIJACKING THE EDUCATION NARRATIVE

The pathway that has been shaping the direction of K–12 education, and now working to establish itself into teacher education, has clearly been hijacked by a corporatized narrative. Disturbingly, the framing of this narrative has been calculatingly influential in swaying many in the general public. As Lakoff (2004) puts it, "That is what framing is about. Framing is about getting language that fits your worldview. It is not just language. The ideas are primary—and the language carries those ideas, evokes those ideas" (p. 4).

We should all be alarmed. And unless there is the will, commitment, and vision to push back on this neoliberal trajectory, it will continue to seep over the entire education profession landscape like *The Blob* in that 1958 sci-fi cult classic that starred the late Steve McQueen. In that film, the blob, a jellylike organism, invades a small community, slithering through the area and consuming anything in its sight, including people, all of which strengthens its power and enlarges its size. McQueen, one of the first witnesses of this creepy glob, warns the townspeople, who were not aware of this creature taking over its community.

In a sense, like the slithering glob, a neoliberal education agenda—with its bottomless coffers, is rapidly expanding. Like the McQueen character, we must simultaneously pay attention and resist, yet not get distracted and lose sight of the internal forces and politics at play within teacher education itself, which we begin with a historical overview. Indeed, to understand the context of where we are and where we are going, we must be aware of the past.

NOTES

1. As a result and unprecedented since the 1960s, it should be no surprise that a "sleeping" giant is waking up, declaring, "Enough!" That is, in 2018 we witnessed teachers in states such as North Carolina, West Virginia, Oklahoma, Arizona, and Colorado speaking out in full force demanding just pay, equitable benefits, and proper funding for curriculum and instruction, and against a test-centric schooling environment. These resistance efforts have caught the attention of policy makers and the general public, perhaps signaling that these efforts are the beginning of critical change.

2. As one examines the data and projections for the future, the shortage of teachers will continue to get worse, particularly exacerbated in special education, mathematics, and science (Sutcher, Darling-Hammond, & Carver-Thomas, 2016). Moreover, while an estimated 20 percent of the teaching population in the United States are teachers of color and of that 2 percent are African American men, "we know that teachers of color leave the profession at a higher rate than their white colleagues" (King & Darling-Hammond, 2018, p. 6).

3. The 2017 federal poverty guidelines for a household of one is $12,060; two is $16,240; three is $20,420; five is $28,780; six is $32,960; seven is $37,140; and eight is $41,320 (see Families USA, 2018).

4. As Sykes (2008) puts it, "The status, wages, and other valuables associated with teaching constitute a final difficulty for teacher education. Teaching has always suffered an equivocal status compounded of respect and disdain, reverence, and mockery" (p. 1296).

5. See Rose's insightful, balanced critique of NCTQ and its relationship with teacher education in Strauss (2014).

6. See Strauss (2015).

7. See *TTU* (2015).

8. See http://www.niet.org/who-we-are/our-mission/. Though several states could serve as an example, the state of Louisiana illustrates how NIET is already working overtime in establishing itself into K–12 education (See https://www.louisianabelieves.com/teaching/tap).

9. Not only did one of us (James) have to endure the training sessions, but also he was in communication with colleagues from Texas Tech University who went

through the same process. Moreover, he communicated with other colleagues at Northern Arizona University who went through training, leading them to release the following work: Wegwert & Foley (2017).

10. See NIET (n.d.).

11. See also Laura Chapman's (2016) thoughtful piece on why we should resist such programs as NIET.

12. In a certain way during this era, there has been an almost complicit, perhaps understandable, passivity from schools of education. With fears of alienating increasingly conservative state legislatures, and with university leaders faced with budget cuts, positions of outcry or counter ideas have been formally muted. Anecdotally, in some cases academic staffs have been "told" to silence their criticisms of policy in order to maintain good relationships with those doing the cutting and with conservative donors (dialogue between James D. Kirylo and John Fischetti, 2018).

III

TEACHER EDUCATION AND THE POLITICS WITHIN

• 5 •

A Rocky Historical Road toward Teacher Education

Before the advent of the common school movement in the 1830s, school-aged youngsters were educated in a variety of settings, such as the home, church, public lectures, and apprenticeships, and depending on the setting, the teachers could have been a parent, a minister, a tutor, or a town official, to name a few.

When the common school movement appeared on the scene in the late 1830s, the need for more teachers became apparent, and the need for some kind of formal teacher preparation program was evident, which prompted the opening of the first normal school (derived from the French *école normale*, a school in which teaching norms or practices were learned) in 1839 in Lexington, Massachusetts.[1]

For Horace Mann and others, the goal of the normal school was to prepare well-educated individuals to become professional teachers. However, these first teacher education programs did not imply university-based work; rather, they were high schools designed to prepare candidates to teach in the common schools as elementary school teachers (Labaree, 2008; Levine, 2006).

The creation of the normal school was driven by a clear sense of mission, viewing the teaching profession in high esteem (Feiman-Nemser, 1990), with the idea that one could "turn the temporary occupation of schoolkeeping into a life-time career of schoolteaching . . . to replace the citizen-teachers with classroom professionals" (Herbst, 1989, p. 140).

Although women had taught basic literacy skills in what was known as dame schools (largely at home settings) before the common school era, it was only during the emergence of the common schools that the feminization of teaching began to unfold. Prior to this time, men were dominantly those who taught, but because of other opportunities for men, the Civil War, and the high need for more teachers, women more and more filled the role as teachers, particularly at the elementary level. Additionally, it was thought that women, with their good morals, their ability to be natural nurturers, and their generally gentler nature compared to men, were better suited to teach (Kincheloe, Slattery, & Steinberg, 2000; Levin, Pinto, McCarthy, Moore, & Scott, n.d.).

Because there were few opportunities for women to be employed, many saw teaching as that window to enter a career, even though they were viewed as second-class citizens, were paid less than men, were not allowed to marry (and were compelled to resign if they married), and certainly were not considered for positions as administrators or school principals (Kincheloe, Slattery, & Steinberg, 2000; Levin et al., n.d.).[2] In short, it is no wonder that Kozol (2009) would proclaim, "For generations women have been treated with contempt, or else relegated wholly to oblivion, within U.S. public schools" (p. 29).

Labaree (2008) points out that while the intent of the normal school was focused on quality, the need for teachers to serve in the common schools outweighed the focus on that element. That is, the quality and time of teacher preparation took a back seat to the interest of relevance in order to churn teachers out to the classrooms.

When it comes to making decisions about teacher preparation programs today, the same mindset continues to erringly persist as that of the mid-1800s.

Labaree (2008) further explains:

> It should surprise no one that normal school leaders ended up choosing relevance over rigor. Doing otherwise would have been difficult. To preserve academic rigor would have meant opting for professional purism over social need; it would have meant leaving mass teacher preparation to less qualified providers; and it would have meant depriving their institutions of the funding, power, and opportunities for expansion that would come with making themselves useful. (p. 293)[3]

Operating on sparse funding, with programs lasting anywhere from a year or two, as the normal schools grew in number across the country, low standards of admission prevailed; minimal rigor with more of a vocational emphasis as opposed to an academic focus was practiced; and programs primarily attracted those candidates who had completed only elementary school. Clearly, the expansion of normal schools was conducted at the expense of the quality and status of the programs (Kincheloe, Slattery, & Steinberg, 2000; Labaree, 2008; Levine, 2006).

Yet the demand for these schools provided opportunity for people who were not geographically close to a university, could not afford to attend the university, or were attracted by the less rigorous admission standards. In other words, the normal school, albeit solely a teacher preparation program, was an alternative for those who otherwise could not attend the university (Labaree, 2008).

In addition, the market called for the normal school to expand its offerings in the liberal arts, which ultimately came at the expense of losing sight of its mission on teacher education. In short, as the normal school expanded its mission, opportunities increased for more people to attend, dubbing the normal school as the people's college (Labaree, 2008).

THE EMERGENCE OF SCHOOLS AND COLLEGES OF EDUCATION

At the turn of the 20th century, while the normal school was rethinking its identity and in light of addressing teacher education for secondary school teacher candidates, admission standards required a high school degree. Moreover, teacher certification degrees came into play, implying that more time was required for teacher preparation, all of which led normal schools to characterize themselves as teachers' colleges (Labaree, 2008; Webb, Metha, & Jordan, 2007).

However, with the diversity of liberal arts programs offered, these colleges—with legislative backing, the raising of requirements, and course work—turned into state colleges. Today colleges and universities all over the country house multiple programs, schools, or colleges, which include colleges of education (Labaree, 2008; Webb, Metha, & Jordan, 2007).

Labaree (2008) additionally makes the point that while normal schools essentially morphed into schools of education, these schools are typically housed at regional universities, and regional universities "reside at the bottom of the university status order" (p. 293). In other words, as compared to Research 1 or state flagship universities, which have a greater emphasis on research and are generally viewed with more prestige, regional universities are generally not viewed in kind.

This, of course, is not to say that Research 1 universities don't have schools or colleges of education, but generally the difference between a teacher education program in a regional university and that of a Research 1 institution is that the former is principally focused on undergraduate teacher preparation while staying closely linked to the local schools, whereas the latter is focused on graduate work, research, and strong academics, with very little time spent on teacher preparation (Labaree, 2008).

The consequence of this phenomenon is that the low status of teacher education is perpetuated—with regional universities on the receiving end of this blow—and comes from a variety of disparate directions such as so-called reformers, professors, and those from the left and the right, part of which "is a legacy of the market pressures that shaped the history of the normal school; in part it is a side effect of the bad company that teacher education is seen as keeping; and in part it is a result of the kind of work that teachers and teacher educators do" (Labaree, 2008, p. 297).

In a recent *Chronicle of Higher Education* report, regional universities in particular have been acutely stretched with exponential budget cuts, the slashing of programs, and falling student enrollment, all of which has made these universities prey to the aforementioned market forces, paving the way for commercial consulting firms to pounce. In this light, many see the eroding away of faculty input and academic integrity (Kelderman, 2014).

Added to the latter reality—and while varying from one teacher education program to another—is the ongoing internal politics teacher education has with itself when it comes to requirements, faculty expectations, and how the hiring process is conducted, which we explore in the following two chapters.

NOTES

1. The inception of formal teacher programs is a relatively new phenomenon, dating back to the mid-1600s with the French Catholic priest Jean-Baptiste de la Salle, who is given many titles, such as founder of the first normal school in Rheims, France, the "father" of student teaching, educational reformer, patron of all teachers, and father of modern pedagogy (Graham, 1910; Guyton & McIntyre, 1990; Sladky, 2014).

2. On average women are still underpaid as compared to men in similar lines of work. It was not until 1920 that women were able to vote in a presidential election.

3. Since the establishment and expansion of the normal school, the United States has been constantly wrangling with the quantity-versus-quality question juxtaposed relative to the debate between whether teaching is a profession or a trade (or what some would call a craft). Therefore, as it is today, with the shortage of teachers coupled with an acute need for qualified teachers to be placed in high-challenging settings, the need has justified a focus on the quantity, which has particularly enabled the point of view that teaching is a trade that simply requires training. This has, therefore, validated for-profit and nonprofit alternative or fast-track programs in which to quickly "prepare" teacher candidates for the classroom. A consequence of this phenomenon is that some states are funding more and more of these types of programs at the expense of depleting even more the already proven traditional teacher education programs despite enduring years of budget cuts/reductions. Furthermore,

the notion of viewing teaching as a trade (or craft) versus a profession disturbingly appears to be dictated by economic class, race, and geographic setting. As Levine (2006) asserts, "It seems that teachers in urban schools would more likely be prepared for a craft than their counterparts in suburban schools. Hard-to-staff subjects would also be more likely to employ teachers educated via alternative routes. Low-income children of color would more likely be taught by teachers educated for a craft than their more affluent white peers. School systems concerned principally with increasing the number of teachers would be more likely to hire faculty prepared for a craft, while school systems emphasizing qualitative improvement would more likely be inclined to recruit teachers prepared for a profession. . . . In deregulating teacher preparation by opening alternative providers, the states and the federal government did away with quality ceilings and floors" (pp. 17, 21).

• 6 •

Sameness versus Difference

Is Teacher Education Clear about Faculty Expectations?

𝓕raser's (1997) model of social justice proposes three pervasive tensions. One of these is "sameness versus difference,"[1] that is, "is equality achieved by working for sameness or is it accomplished by valuing difference?" (Aldridge, Christensen, & Emfinger, 2010, p. 377).

Federal legislation appears to support both sameness and difference. For example, the No Child Left Behind Act (NCLB) of 2001 was created to close the gap between low-income and middle-income schools by creating sameness. Students in special groups, such as English-language learners or children in special education, are expected to meet the same standards as everyone else. *Accommodations* may be made to help students meet the standards, but everyone is expected to meet the same standards.

Contrast this with the Individuals with Disabilities Education Improvement Act of 2004 (IDEA), which was created to promote social justice and equity in curriculum by emphasizing difference. Students with special needs receive an individual education plan to meet their unique needs because they are different. *Accommodations* or *modifications* are made based on how different a student is from his or her peers.

To that end and in a parallel way to the above, the sameness-versus-difference tension can be found with respect to (1) faculty expectations—namely, the triad of teaching, research, and service; and (2) compensation and the hiring process.

Tenure earning or tenured faculties in colleges of education are expected to work in the areas of *teaching*, *research*, and *service*. But should the same standards apply to all faculty members? For example, many colleges of education set the standard at 1/3 teaching, 1/3 research, and 1/3 service. This promotes sameness in expectations for all faculty members. However, many faculty members argue that their strengths are in one of the three areas and it should be weighted higher than the other two. These individuals are promoting difference in "weighting" and evaluation based on the strengths of each faculty member.

While concepts related to curriculum and instruction will be discussed later, the issue of sameness versus difference in *teaching* is important to mention here because of what teacher education programs decide to promote. North (2008) explains that sameness/difference should not be a dichotomy. She suggests that it is not "either/or" but "both/and."

Still, most education programs lean in one direction or the other. For example, the answer to the question "Does everyone learn the same way, just at different rates of learning, or are there specific learning styles that are different from one student to another?" is still being debated.

There are those who strongly believe in specific learning styles or specific types of intelligences (Gardner, 2008; Peterson & Kolb, 2017). Yet there are also proponents that say there is no research evidence to support learning styles (Newton & Miah, 2017). While many colleges have proponents of both, it is not uncommon to find that a respective college of education has more proponents of one perspective over those of the other.

Evaluating the effectiveness of faculty teaching in colleges of education has also presented challenges. Should all teachers be evaluated in the same way, or are there different ways to "measure" teaching? While multiple forms of teaching effectiveness should be used, many schools of education have relied heavily on student evaluations of professors, using a Likert scale.

On one hand, teacher educators who entertain, are slightly to moderately demanding, and help students "feel comfortable" tend to be rated higher by students. On the other hand, teacher educators who challenge students academically but also ask students to question their core beliefs tend to make students uncomfortable. However, higher education, including teacher education, should instigate dissonance and conflict in student thinking, which is not often viewed favorably by students.

Research is also continuously deliberated in teacher education programs regarding the sameness/difference continuum. What constitutes good research? For several decades a dissonance has existed between quantitative and qualitative supporters. One faculty member at an unnamed university expressed this tension as follows:

> The quantitative researchers at my university say that qualitative research should not be considered research. They say qualitative researchers grab a pen and paper or an iPad and go out to the schools and see what develops. They have no idea what they are doing and this should not be valued as much as rigorous quantitative studies. The qualitative researchers say the

quantitative faculty are nothing but number-crunching behaviorists who do not consider the context or thick, rich descriptions necessary for understanding educational problems and practices.

This same faculty member suggested quantitative and qualitative methods should be used together. For example, after preliminary quantitative results are determined, qualitative methods can be used to consider outliers or qualitative questions designed as a follow-up.

Can an education program determine what is and is not good research? If so, are both quantitative and qualitative research considered "equally"? This question is a loaded one in that quantitative research has historically been associated with male dominance and qualitative research has been considered a more feminine approach (Fee, 1986; Lincoln & Guba, 1985; Ramazanoglu & Holland, 2002).

During the era of NCLB, teaching practices were expected to be based on "scientific research," which largely implied randomized experimental studies, suggesting the "gold standard for determining cause and effect" (Reyna, 2004, p. 52). And lower and unacceptable forms of research included quasi-experiments, correlational studies, and case studies, as a "single case study can lead to mistaken generalizations" (p. 52). Furthermore, it was the researchers, not the teachers, who were to translate the scientific research into practical applications for classroom use (Reyna, 2004).

Beyond the federal government's definition of scientifically based research, many teacher education programs rank journals into tiers as to which ones are required or recommended as quality research journals. The journals that are ranked the highest tend to promote quantitative research over qualitative. So are faculty members expected to be the same, publishing in Research 1 journals that are quantitative? Or are different forms of research accepted and valued as good research for faculty evaluation and movement toward tenure and promotion?

Service is also a requirement of most teacher education faculties. Are most professors expected to do similar service, or are a wide range of service options encouraged? Most faculties are expected to do some service at the international/national, state, and local levels as well as service within the college.

However, this sameness of expectations is not always the case, and it can change from one year to the next. One faculty member remembers how her school of education encouraged and supported international service. She took a sabbatical and spent a semester in Eastern Europe doing service and conducting research.

When this faculty member returned to campus, she expected to share her experience with her colleagues. Yet at the first general faculty meeting of the next school year, the dean reported that service expectations were to be focused on the local schools. Anything beyond 100 miles of the college was not encouraged. The baffled faculty member wondered how service expectations had suddenly gone from international to "down the street."

NOTE

1. Nancy Fraser is a feminist, a poststructuralist, and a critical theorist who teaches at the New School in New York City. Her work centers on social justice issues, posing challenging questions about micro/macro, sameness/difference, and recognition/redistribution themes related to the social sciences and education.

· 7 ·

Sameness versus Difference

Is Teacher Education Fair about Compensation and the Hiring Process?

While issues of sameness/difference influence the *teaching*, *research*, and *service* of faculty, sameness/difference issues are also particularly salient when it comes to compensation or annual increases in salaries. Most Research 1 universities (universities with highest research activity) are merit based. The focus is on difference. Those who perform better in teaching, research, and service receive higher merit raises—supposedly.

Since teaching, research, and service cannot be exactly measured, errors can be made and "office politics" sometimes come into play. The pay difference among education faculty members is sometimes astounding because those brought in at lower salaries are at a disadvantage every time raises are given. Obviously, 5 percent of $60,000 is not the same as 5 percent of $120,000. Over time, faculty salaries become more and more disparate.[1]

Another issue related to faculty compensation is the fact that faculty salaries are often based on market value. So faculty members in educational leadership or administration tend to make higher salaries than those in curriculum and instruction because a principal or superintendent makes a higher salary than elementary/secondary teachers. This market value is especially stark when salaries of education faculty members are compared with others across the university.

Medicine, engineering, business, and law professors command substantially higher salaries than those in education. Education faculty members sometimes fare better than teachers in art, music, and languages. Some smaller universities do focus more on sameness and base compensation more on degree, rank, and years of experience with little room for merit. Faculty pay, however, at these schools tends to be lower than at Research 1 universities.

Hiring practices in colleges and departments of education, as well as in K–12 schools, are also affected by the issue of sameness/difference. A university setting presumably fosters diversity. And while many universities make a concerted effort to hire underrepresented populations, there are subtle prejudices in employment opportunities that are always at work in both higher education and K–12 schools. And this seems to have increased in recent years, as we later give an example of two kindergarten teachers.

Even in rural teachers' colleges in the past, faculty members were hired with degrees from Columbia, Chicago, Peabody, and UCLA. There is now a tendency for some education programs to "hire their own." Today, in several colleges of education, including some at research 1 universities, more than half of the faculties are graduates of the university. As Karger (2016) explains, this sometimes occurs because a job-seeking candidate from another university has only a short time to impress the search committee. They are in competition with someone who has been in the department as a student for years. Further, enthusiastic mentors tend to push their advisees into such positions.

Although subtle and not openly discussed, faculty search committees are in tune with what political party a candidate endorses, and what philosophies they subscribe to (e.g., behaviorism, constructivism, postmodernism, critical pedagogy, multiple intelligences, etc.) and sometimes tend to favor their own graduates. For example, when Condoleezza Rice was provost at Stanford, one faculty member commented that she was happy to have a woman and delighted to have an African American as provost but she did not like the fact that Rice was Republican.

Sameness/difference tensions can be seen on two levels in hiring practices for faculties of education and even in K–12 public schools. One is *external* sameness/difference, and the other is *ideological* sameness/difference. While external characteristics such as age, weight, height, and perceived physical attractiveness are superficial, they do make a difference on who gets favored for employment. Consider this K–12 example: A professor at an urban university agreed to provide continual professional development in literacy during the entire school year for a rural school system, 90 miles from the campus. Two kindergarten teachers in the rural school system requested to see best kindergarten practices in a model class. The professor, therefore, took them to observe a kindergarten teacher near the university. And while the children and their teacher were at lunch, the rural teachers met with the professor to discuss what they had observed. Expecting comments about the curriculum and the teacher's interactions with the children, the professor was stunned when both of the visiting teachers' first comments were, "We could never teach at this school." The professor asked, "Why?" One said, "Because

I am too fat." The other exclaimed, "Because I am too old." The professor asked, "What do you mean?" One of the women explained, "Look around. The school looks like a beauty pageant. All of the teachers are young and blonde and attractive." When the professor commented on this to the kindergarten teacher at the school, she replied, "Yes, the principal does tend to hire the same type."

Ideological sameness also pervades many education programs and K–12 schools. Some programs prefer to hire constructivists, some critical pedagogues, while a few prefer to employ more behaviorist-oriented instructors. Over time, philosophies evolve, but the practice of hiring ideologically similar colleagues seems to remain stable. For example, in the 1980s, the whole language-versus-skills approach to reading wars certainly affected who was offered a job in literacy at many colleges and universities.

Related to concepts that intersect the ideological is whether teacher candidates should be prepared to teach at the macro or micro level, a theme that is discussed in the following chapter.

NOTE

1. It is true, however, that at some university settings when there is a disparity in salaries from new hires coming in at relatively high salaries compared to the salaries of those who have been there for several years, salaries are adjusted for the latter with what is called salary compression.

• 8 •

The Macro versus Micro Challenge

The notion of preparing teacher candidates with a macro-level focus (e.g., what occurs at the national level) and a micro-level focus (e.g., what occurs at the local level) is always a tension that is invariably played out at teacher education programs. Of course, the short answer is that programs must address both levels and everything in between. That is, at the macro level we must ask, Who is in charge of teacher education? Does the power reside at the federal and state levels? How much power does a university or college teacher education program have?

At the micro level, how much autonomy does a teacher educator or K–12 teacher have? And how are both administrative structures at the macro level and teaching practices at the micro level implemented? Does the direction of power flow from the top down, as with Reagan's "trickle-down" economic scheme, or does the power build from the bottom up? Is it possible for power to be shared equally in teacher education among K–12 personnel, teacher education faculty, and administrators? These questions will be explored at both *administrative levels* and *teaching practices* in higher education and K–12 schools.

ADMINISTRATIVE LEVELS

Who controls the power over teacher education and public schools at the administrative level? The federal government, particularly under Republican administrations, has suggested that the power should be located at the local level. This is especially ironic when one of the most comprehensive federal interventions was No Child Left Behind (NCLB), administered as a top-down paradigm during the George W. Bush years (Aldridge, Kilgo, & Emfinger, 2010).

However, it must also be pointed out that Barack Obama's Race to the Top program was one that can be characterized as NCLB on steroids, which included great favor toward establishing charter schools and a carrot-stick approach to education by dangling federal dollars in order to gain compliance to a prescriptive approach to schooling (Kirylo, 2011). To be sure, the Right, however, has largely led the charge in promoting charter schools, despite the valid criticism that the charter school network works to defund traditional public schools, even close them, and fosters resegregation.

Through the U.S. Department of Education, federal funds are distributed to the states and grant money is available for programs in higher and K–12 education, particularly in special education. Furthermore, the Council for the Accreditation of Educator Preparation (CAEP), a national organization (to be discussed in the next chapter), determines which teacher education programs are accredited. These are just a few of many examples of top-down administration influencing both teacher education and K–12 schools. Yet, financially poorer schools are especially vulnerable to top-down policies. So-called failing schools may be taken over by the State Department of Education and thus are more likely to be required to administer a scripted curriculum.

Suffice it to say, the vast majority of teacher education programs and K–12 schools are influenced in some form by a top-down administration. As power supposedly trickles down from the top, less and less power occurs at the local level, similar to what happens in a trickle-down economy.

TEACHING PRACTICES

The macro-versus-micro debate also influences pedagogical practices in K–12 schools and higher education. Should instruction be delivered from the top down or from the bottom up? In the last two decades of the 20th century, a highly contentious debate pervaded literacy instruction and was often referred to as the "whole to part" (whole language) versus the "part to whole" (skills/phonics) debate (Goodman, 2014). This debate, like many education tensions, is an ideological matter.

However, Bank Street College of Education and School for Children in New York City proposed a convincing approach for teaching young children, moving from micro to macro levels. This is still known as a "here and now" approach to learning (Antler, 1987; Mitchell, 1916; Nager & Shapiro, 2007). That is, in answering the question "Where do you begin to teach young children?" Mitchell (1916) proposed that one always begin with the "here and now" and move outward.

In other words, teachers begin with the microsystem of the child and teach outward toward the macrosystem. The teacher and children begin by exploring each other's names and then the classroom. They continue by investigating the school and neighborhood, and over a considerable length of time they study their community, town, state, nation, and beyond.

The "here and now" curriculum sounds like common sense, but it is not uncommon that scores of preschool and kindergarten teachers do not teach the "here and now." For example, in a rural southern state, a preschool teacher of children in poverty had the children study the rain forest and, later, polar bears. Directly across the street from her school/classroom was a strip mall containing a hardware store, a bakery, a grocery store, and a pizza parlor. When a teacher educator asked why the children were learning about rain forests and polar bears instead of exploring the richness of the immediate neighborhood, the teacher looked baffled and could not answer. Do we want children to study rain forests and polar bears? Of course—but not before they have explored their local ecology. Beginning with the micro level and moving toward the macro level can be achieved through a "here and now approach."

In a similar way the "where do you begin to instruct teacher candidates" has plagued teacher education for decades. That is, in the past, teacher education majors studied "how to teach" before they had even observed in a classroom. Through CAEP and State Department requirements, teacher candidates are required to have extensive observation and participation in public schools. However, in some cases, students are supposedly learning how to teach before they have observed in a classroom. Again, it would appear that intensive observation and participation should be required before studying extensively how to teach.

In the end, curriculum and instruction courses should involve students in observation and participation as part of learning "what to teach" and "how to teach." However, methods courses differ from state to state because each state is responsible for determining course requirements and certification standards, as we will discuss in the following chapter.

· 9 ·

Two-Stepping among Colleges of Education, Accrediting Agencies, and State Departments of Education

In the United States, decisions about education in general and teacher education in particular have been the responsibility of each individual state. That means decisions about teacher education programs and the certification of teachers and paraprofessionals have been different from Hawaii to Maine. Each state sets its own standards and requirements.

However, overriding this autonomy has been a national accreditation system, namely, the National Council for Accreditation of Teacher Education (NCATE), which dominated accreditation for decades, and now the Council for the Accreditation of Educator Preparation (CAEP), which has taken the lead (Heafner, McIntyre, & Spooner, 2014).

During the 1970s, NCATE accreditation was considered by many teacher educators as a good thing. For one, students who graduated from an NCATE-approved program could easily get a teacher's certificate in another state. There were 45+ states that provided reciprocity in teacher certification if a student from another state had graduated from an NCATE-approved program. However, over time this reciprocity was chipped away, and getting a teacher's certificate in another state became increasingly difficult. Further, NCATE began increasing requirements and standards, signaling a desire for more control.

For example, consider how most teacher education programs claim to live by some variation of the motto "teacher as reflective decision maker" even though most decisions in teacher education programs are already made for the teacher candidates. That is, as opposed to times past, education majors were given several elective options in planning their course of study.

Today, however, essentially every course is prescribed with only perhaps one elective, though more commonly no possibility for electives. Virtually no autonomous decisions can be made by students themselves. Why? Because

CAEP and the below-discussed state departments of education have cultivated an environment whereby students have few or no choices except to follow an endless list of competencies and course requirements that must be met. In the same vein as a the previous discussion, sameness prevails.

Ironically, however, also in times past, some outstanding teacher education programs were not NCATE accredited. For example, the earlier mentioned Bank Street College of Education in New York City opted out for years, even though they are now accredited. Furthermore, highly ranked Research 1 universities, such as UCLA and the University of Wisconsin (Madison) are not currently listed as NCATE or CAEP accredited on the CAEP official website (CAEP, 2018).

While NCATE and now CAEP have been highly praised by some and greatly criticized by others, suffice it to say the national accreditation of teacher education programs has been and remains highly controversial and among the primary continuing tensions within teacher education.

Relative to the above, typically state departments of education develop their standards around national standards (Korthagen, 2001). Certification requirements are set, and teacher education programs must meet state department standards and students must complete a state-approved program in their subject/program area in order to be certified. Beyond this, the relationship between school, colleges, and departments of education and their state's department of education are vastly different from one state to another. The following are two examples from different states regarding this relationship.

State names have been withheld because the purpose is not to criticize or praise specific states but to emphasize the disparity in the way teacher certification is administered. In one state, the state certification officer and staff at the Department of Education involve all of the colleges and universities that have teacher education programs in setting certification standards. Faculties from each program around the state work together with the Department of Education. In essence, the faculty members who know and teach education classes develop the certification requirements.

Of course there are numerous considerations such as national accreditation policies and PRAXIS test requirements. Still, teacher education faculties in this state are considered the "experts," and the State Department of Education relies heavily on their expertise. When a student's transcript and other documentation are sent to the State Department for the student to receive a teaching certificate, the State Department personnel respect and usually accept the college or university's request for the student. Course substitutions and other variations are seldom questioned. In the vernacular, when a college certification officer says to a State Department certification official, "Send Mary her teacher's certificate," the process usually goes smoothly and Mary gets her certificate.

The above example is quite different from that of another state. In this second State Department of Education, the person in charge of teacher education and certification runs the department with an iron fist. Faculty input purportedly exists in this state. Faculties of education from around the state are members of respective committees to provide input, but the end result is that the head state certification officer makes all the decisions. And in implementation of state-approved programs, he does not allow for the slightest clerical error.

For example, one student registered for the wrong course number when taking a required education course, even though she took the correct class. The course was cross-listed with another course, and she simply chose the wrong number required by her certification checklist. The State Department sent it back to the university and said the student would have to take the course again.

In response, the university faculty advisor indicated the student took the correct course but just signed up for the wrong course number. State Department certification personnel demanded the faculty member write a letter explaining the mistake, and the professor was expected to grovel, beg for forgiveness, and explain that this error would not happen again.

The above very real scenario is particularly dehumanizing and deprofessionalizing of teacher education faculties, especially when the state certification officer does not have a background in education (not to mention the secretary of education for the United States has no educational background). Such nonsense is one of the main reasons that for many, teacher certification has a "Mickey Mouse" reputation.

What was once a good idea has become a nightmare. Teacher education and certification has become a seemingly unlimited documentation trail—more and more standards, seemingly endless additional PRAXIS and edTPA tests requirements, coupled with expensive and commercially produced programs that are required to present documented evidence (Korthagen, 2004).

All of these are "shiny objects" designed to distract teachers and keep them from advocating for themselves and their students. This is ironic when a prestigious Harvard professor of history would not qualify for a history teaching job in a rural Mississippi middle school because she did not meet the requirements for a teacher's certificate (Humphrey, Wechsler, & Hough, 2008).

To be sure, some state departments of education work collaboratively and cooperatively with teacher education programs. They listen to education faculties throughout their state and incorporate their ideas and suggestions. Others have become the tail that wags the dog. Yet teacher education faculties' knowledge and professionalism are needed in local, state, and national dialogues concerning accreditation and certification. Simply by increasing the quantity of standards has not proven to increase the quality of teaching. More is not better.

• *10* •

Quantity versus Quality in Accepting Teacher Candidates

*A*nother tension facing teacher education is the "quantity versus quality" question, that is, the number of students versus the quality of students admitted. Many teacher education programs are "cash cows" for the university, and university administrators want as many students as possible. This particularly comes at a time when state legislatures have systematically worked to defund higher education, placing an exacerbated burden on students. In short, universities are more and more becoming tuition-driven enterprises.

While the teacher education literature abounds espousing the salience of equal opportunity and access to education and social capital for *all* students, this does not suggest that anyone can become a teacher (Anyon, 2005; Apple, 2000; Delpit, 1995; Freire, 1990; Gutmann, 1999; Kozol, 2005; Lynch & Baker, 2005; McDonald, 2003; Tye, 2000; Young, 1990). What it does signify, however, is that everyone regardless of age, race, ethnicity, religion, gender, nationality, sexual orientation, or ability should have an equal opportunity access to teacher education programs.

To be sure, the reality and results of an open-door policy are not ideal for any stakeholder. For example, teacher education programs are often judged on "exit scores" of their graduates and given grades by their respective state departments of education. Open-door policy programs are likely to result in a heightened decrease in standardized measures relative to assessing and evaluating respective teacher education programs. In short, open-door policies often result in lower teacher performance scores, thus giving the school a lesser reputation than more selective programs.

On the other hand, teacher education programs that are highly selective have neglected and marginalized historically disenfranchised groups. This will continue to happen unless they intentionally recruit and retain students who are typically underrepresented in teacher education programs, such as Black, Asian, and Latino males (Christensen & Aldridge, 2013). And since universities have been "forced" to corporatize with a business-model approach, the upper administration is more than likely to frown upon the lack of student enrollment, meaning lack of tuition dollars coming in.

What university administrators—via the pressure of respective state legislatures—really want is both quantity *and* quality: a large number of students who are the "cream of the crop." This is an extreme challenge, to say the least (Aldridge & Goldman, 2007). This challenge results in another continuing tension in teacher education that requires continuous dialogue among all stakeholders, thoughtfully considered at each individual teacher education program and one that permeates an air that works to recruit, retain, and support underrepresented populations (Ladson-Billings, 1994).

IV

THE QUESTION OF WHAT AND HOW TO TEACH

• *11* •

The Relationship between Curriculum and Instruction

*T*urning points and new directions in teacher education will always influence decisions concerning curriculum and instruction. "What to teach" and "how to teach" are hallmarks of teacher education that have been debated since the advent of teacher education programs. While "teaching methods" were briefly touched on earlier, this chapter focuses solely on dialogues about what to teach and how to teach.

As one examines the literature on curriculum, there are more than 100 definitions of what it is and how it functions. In the spirit of a Tylerian model of our understanding of curriculum,[1] Oliva (2009) argues, "Curriculum is built, planned, designed, and constructed. It is improved, revised, and evaluated. Like photographic film and muscles, the curriculum is developed. It is also organized, structured, restructured, and, like a wayward child, reformed" (p. 3). If what is taught is called curriculum, then instruction is not the same thing. Instruction is *how* curriculum is implemented.[2] So what is the interconnection between curriculum and instruction?

In one of the most comprehensive explanations made about the relationship between curriculum and instruction, Oliva (2009) argues that this relationship can be described in four ways: *dualistic, interlocking, concentric,* and *cyclical* conceptions.

Those who support a *dualistic* conception believe there is no relationship between curriculum and instruction. Curriculum "planners ignore the instructors and in turn are ignored by them" (Oliva, 2009, p. 8). Throughout history, the federal and state governments have developed and evaluated the effectiveness of curricula without input from the instructors. For example, consider the 15-member National Reading Panel formed at the end of the 20th century.

The panel was organized to "assess the status of research-based knowledge, including the effectiveness of various approaches to teaching children to read" (Yatvin, 2003, p. 36). Of the 15 members, all were scientists with the exception of Joanne Yatvin, a public school principal. Yatvin noted that "as time went on, I saw that the opinion of the panel's scientists always carried more weight than those of the rest of us. Panel decisions repeatedly demonstrated that experience working in schools with children . . . was not highly valued" (Yatvin, 2003, p. 37).

Interlocking conceptions of curriculum and instruction supports the belief that both are entwined and connected in the shape of a Venn diagram. They influence one another, but there is really no emphasis or discussion favoring one or the other. In fact, it is just assumed that there is some type of relationship between the two, but this relationship is not addressed. It is assumedly lodged in the unconscious when planners and teachers discuss curriculum and instruction, meaning there is an inherent understood relationship, realizing to separate "one from the other would do serious harm to both" (Oliva, 2009, p. 9).

Concentric beliefs about curriculum show the instruction circle within curriculum or the curriculum circle embedded in the instruction circle. In other words, mutual dependence is acknowledged, with one being more important than the other, depending on which circle contains the other. While both are vital, inextricably connected, and salient, one is seen as more important than the other. Is what we teach more important than how we teach, or should how we teach take the lead over what we teach?

Cyclical notions promote a reciprocal relationship between curriculum and instruction. Supporters of cyclical conceptions believe that what is taught will influence how it is taught and how instruction is delivered will support and modify the content that is taught. For example, some content must be taught directly, such as language and the names of things. Other content, such as sports, is taught through direct, physical action.

The question of *content* versus *methods* will continue in teacher education because a propensity for one over another is an ideological concern. There are those at one extreme who believe that majors such as "elementary education" or "administration" should not be allowed to exist because they have no content; they believe these majors are about process rather than content. For example, elementary education students must teach content (e.g., literacy, math, science, and social studies) and therefore should have a major in one of these "content" areas. This is also true of "administration." Administration of what? What are the "content" principals are expected to administer?

At the other extreme are those who believe that if an individual is an expert in content then that should automatically qualify the individual for teaching. At the university level, this is certainly the case, since all nonteacher education faculty members hold advanced degrees but have virtually no background in teaching methods and have typically not obtained a teaching certificate. Moreover, many education faculty members themselves do not hold K–12 teaching certificates.

Some education programs advertise for faculty in special education that requires a "doctoral degree in special education, developmental psychology, or related field." However, there is no reciprocity in developmental psychology. Faculty in psychology would never support a developmental psychology colleague with a terminal degree in special education. For example, there are no advertisements for developmental psychology positions that say, "doctorate in developmental psychology, special education, or related field."

In short, decision making about curriculum and instruction can be complex and "messy." Whatever decisions are made about the relationship between the two, the process always involves political decisions at some level, as shown above with the example of the National Reading Panel. What is taught and how it is taught is always the result of an ideological or political agenda.

NOTES

1. While curriculum as a formal field of studies appeared on the scene in 1918, it was Ralph Tyler's 1949 book *Basic Principles of Curriculum and Instruction*, with its emphasis on such concepts as goals and objectives, that has been highly influential in facilitating our understanding of the curriculum up to this day. However, it is equally important to note that while Tyler's influence on curriculum development cannot be ignored, the postmodern curriculum development paradigm, which hones in on the autobiographical narrative, challenges the traditional Tylerian model (Slattery, 1995). Beginning in the 1970s, a powerful movement to reconceptualize the meaning and action of curriculum emerged as a result of, among the scholarship of others, William Pinar's etymological examination of *currere*, the Latin infinitive verb of the word *curriculum* (Pinar & Grumet, 1976; Pinar, Reynolds, Slattery, & Taubman, 1995). *Currere* implies running a race, meaning that curriculum is not seen as something tangible, as in the case of the articulation of goals and objectives. Rather, curriculum is an activity, an inward autobiographical journey, affecting the direction of the schooling experience. In other words, curriculum work must be historically contextualized, explored, and negotiated, all of which must be linked to conceptions of emancipation (Giroux, 1988).

2. As a point of distinction between pedagogy and instruction, the former indicates the art and science of teaching, which is concretely expressed through the latter (i.e., the instructional approach taken by the teacher). The suggested difference, therefore, between pedagogy and instruction implies that the concept *pedagogy* is driven by a point of view, a belief system, and a philosophy of teaching, and *instruction* is the carrying out of that philosophy in action (Kirylo, 2016b; Koch, 2009).

• *12* •

Models, Approaches, and Frameworks

What's the Difference?

*C*urricula can be divided into three broad areas, which include *models, approaches,* and *frameworks*. Because many curriculum planners and textbooks often use these concepts interchangeably (Aldridge, Emfinger, & Martin, 2006), here we make the distinction clear in order to better our understanding of the relationship between curriculum and instruction.

MODELS

A curriculum *model* is very distinct because it involves a script from which teachers should not vary. Developers of *models* are proud to report that the curriculum is "teacher proof." No decisions need to be made by the teachers except to follow the script. So much for "teaching as reflective decision maker!" An example of *models* would be the earlier-mentioned scientifically based research curricula under No Child Left Behind (NCLB).

In most cases, teachers were not allowed to veer from the script and not permitted to add additional instruction or modify the script in any way. This would influence the fidelity of treatment. Fidelity of treatment was interpreted by some states and school districts in the strictest sense. The result was the establishment of what some teachers called the "fidelity of treatment" police in many school systems.

For example, in Florida, teachers were troubled by "their schools' use of a pacing calendar to prescribe topics and timelines so that all teachers cover the same material at the same time each day. They spoke of unannounced visits by administrators in their classrooms to monitor compliance with the pacing calendar" (Harper, Platt, Naranjo, & Boynton, 2007, p. 647).

In essence, a curriculum *model* is analogous to a fundamentalist religion. Every action is to be followed by the book. A model, just like most fundamentalist ideologies, is a closed system in which most knowledge and information outside of the model are ignored or discouraged. Models are most often supported by a conservative agenda. Supposedly, information and types of knowledge are carefully controlled for the "betterment" of learning. That is why models are (1) scripted, (2) "teacher proofed," and (3) expected to be followed to the letter. They subscribe to a mechanistic paradigm and are behaviorist in theory.

APPROACHES

Approaches provide explicit guidelines with regard to curriculum and instruction, but they are unlike models in one very important way. Approaches are not meant to be replicated exactly from one context to the next. In other words, there are no scripted approaches. If a curriculum is scripted, it is not an approach. Most approaches are concerned with teaching students to think for themselves and make connections in their learning. This is different from models that are usually interested in the "correct answer."

A teacher who teaches using an approach rather than a model sometimes says, "I would rather a student get a wrong answer using correct reasoning than get a correct answer using faulty reasoning." The Developmental-Interaction or Bank Street Approach is one example (Nager & Shapiro, 2007). Other examples include the Project Approach (Katz & Chard, 2000; Kilpatrick, 1918; Lickey & Powers, 2011) and some state department of education curriculum guides that are specific but not scripted (Aldridge & Goldman, 2007).

Politically, approaches tend to be supported by more moderate to liberal groups, since materials are not "teacher proof" as they are designed to be in models. The teacher is considered a professional who makes decisions based on the context, informed judgment, and interactions with the students.

FRAMEWORKS

A framework is a general set of guidelines proposed by a professional organization or group of associates that describes the most basic curriculum and ways to deliver instruction. While content may be addressed in a framework, the focus of a framework is usually on the "process" of instruction.

Examples of frameworks can be found in the following works: *Best Practices* (Zemelman, Daniels, & Hyde, 1998), *Developmentally Appropriate Practice in Early Childhood Programs Serving Children from Birth through Age 8* (Copple & Bredekamp, 2009), *Developmentally Appropriate Middle Level Schools* (Manning, 2002), and *DEC Recommended Practices: A Comprehensive Guide for Practical Application in Early Intervention/Early Childhood Special Education* (Sandall, Hemmeter, Smith, & McLean, 2005). Bloom's taxonomy can also be used as a framework (Bloom, Englehart, Furst, Hill, & Karthwohl, 1956).

Instead of being distinctly separate, *models, approaches,* and *frameworks* are interconnected, and it is often difficult to tell the difference from one to another. Further, some teachers use frameworks as if they were models, and others take models and modify them to meet their needs, disregarding the scripted nature of the curriculum. In reality, *models, approaches,* and *frameworks* are never "pure." For example, there are constructivist frameworks, but there are also specific constructivist approaches; however, there are no constructivist models since constructivism is antithetical to scripted instruction.

If models, approaches, and frameworks are "muddy," then why should we address them in teacher education? Rather than wasting time trying to determine if a curriculum is a model, an approach, or a framework, should we not address more important issues? Of course, the reason for presenting, discussing, and debating models, approaches, and frameworks is to determine what guidelines are necessary in teacher education in order to promote best practices.

• *13* •

How Should We Teach?

Transmission, Transaction, or Transformation

Although there are thousands of curriculum guides available for teachers and teacher candidates, most teaching methods fall into one of three categories: transmission, transaction, or transformation (Aldridge & Goldman, 2007; Jungck & Marshall, 1992).

TRANSMISSION

Transmission involves the teacher as dispenser of knowledge, whereby students are vessels in which information is poured. The act of transmission goes hand in hand with scripted lessons, even coming in the form of following a teacher's manual. Although this type of methodology is not the most encouraged among teacher educators, it still necessarily plays a essential role in the teaching and learning process.

For example, at the primary grade level, learning the names of objects often comes through some form of transmission, as do characters of a language or the alphabet. Because there are mutually agreed upon conventions of language, we cannot expect students to invent their own language. Language must be transmitted in some form.

Teachers who use only transmission or teach in a transmissive format most of the time are technicians. Today transmission relies heavily on technology. Students are placed on their "appropriate instructional level" and use commercially produced, computer-generated lessons that are often presented in a lockstep fashion.

Particularly for new teachers, transmission is the easiest and more straightforward form of teaching. Parents and caregivers understand transmission because generally they were taught at one time through transmission. Guardians remember worksheets, workbooks, and traditional forms of homework. Transmission is easy to document and measure. Indeed, as Christensen and Aldridge (2013) argue, transmission is "the most common type of teaching throughout the world today" (p. 71).

However, there are many drawbacks with transmission. For instance, students are not encouraged to think for themselves and real-world problem solving is lacking. Transmission does not promote oral language learning or interactions that are salient for learners, especially English-language learners and children with special needs. Transmission classrooms are usually expected to be quiet, while students work individually without collaborating. In most cases, collaboration is considered cheating in transmission environments.

Transmission also marginalizes teachers. When teachers are demanded to teach through transmission using a script and every teacher is to be on the same page at the same time, then the teacher's role is compliance with this oppression if she or he wants a good evaluation and to survive. We have already mentioned the "fidelity of treatment police" used during the No Child Left Behind (NCLB) era when teachers had "unannounced visits by administrators in their classrooms to monitor the compliance with the pacing calendar" (Harper, Platt, Naranjo, & Boynton, 2007, p. 647).

At the university level, online classes often rely too heavily on transmission. Faculty members who primarily require students to read a chapter and take a test without interaction or reflection focus on transmission teaching. Thus, one of the biggest problems with transmission teaching is that it does not move individuals toward transaction or transformation.

TRANSACTION

A second general method of teaching is transaction. Transaction is different from transmission because "knowledge is seen as constructed and reconstructed by those participating in the teaching-learning act" (Jungck & Marshall, 1992, p. 94). With transaction, both the teachers and students have more choices in learning.

The teacher will still follow a course of study or curriculum guide, but students work in groups. They share ideas and participate in activities that are "more open-ended and promote higher-level thinking. Students can choose among various ways to represent what they have learned" (Aldridge & Goldman, 2007, p. 109). Transaction has been referred to by other names such as a generative model (Wink, 2011) and as a constructivist approach (Kamii,

2000). Transaction is encouraged in several curriculum approaches, including the Bank Street Approach (Nager & Shapiro, 2007).

Teachers have a vital role in transaction. "While the teacher's role is to teach the prescribed curriculum, she also has the responsibility of promoting social interaction, selecting materials for students to research, and encouraging students to represent what they have learned in novel ways" (Christensen & Aldridge, 2013, p. 75). Students are encouraged or required to work with others as they move toward a common goal. With transaction, the process is often more important than the product. The following is an example of transaction teaching and learning.

Ms. Nissen's fifth-grade students are studying Native American nations. This is part of the prescribed curriculum. However, she divides the class into groups of four and gives each group a native nation in which the group is to become expert. Students in each group research their tribe. They share power and information. One student collects books from the library. Two in the group search the Internet for information. Another student in the group coordinates resources that the teacher has provided. After sharing information with one another, the group decides how best to represent the information they have learned. One group decides to do a mural. Another group plans a fact sheet, and another group decides to perform a skit or play (Aldridge & Goldman, 2007, p. 109).

As this example shows, materials in transaction are more authentic than those used in transmission. "Instead of a worksheet, workbook, or standardized test, students show what they have learned through representation. There are hundreds of ways students can choose to represent what they have learned . . . a web page, an overhead, a fact sheet, a mobile, a game, or a mural or choose numerous other ways to show what they have learned" (Christensen & Aldridge, 2013, p. 76).

Advantages of transaction are many. One of the most important is oral language discussion. This is vital for second-language learners and students with special needs who actively interact with other classmates. All students are involved in some form of research and they are expected to learn in-depth, specific content. Students are given the opportunity to be reflective decision makers, and higher-level thinking is encouraged through transaction (Bloom et al., 1956).

As with all teaching methods, there are drawbacks to transaction teaching. Teachers may not have the management skills or knowledge to implement transaction. Continual decision making is a priority in transaction teaching, and the ability to do this develops over time. As a result, new teachers are often overwhelmed by transaction teaching unless they have a strong mentor or support system to encourage them.

Furthermore, transaction requires a tremendous amount of resources and the ability to manage these resources. Accountability is also a problem in the 21st century. School systems, as well as the federal government and state governments, favor transmission forms of accountability. This is particularly true in special education, and working with students who come from historically disenfranchised populations, upholding "scientifically validated curricula and programs . . . [and] . . . implementing them with fidelity are necessary to ensure the validity of the responsiveness to intervention process" (Fuchs et al., 2007, p. 58).

Finally, covering large amounts of material in short amounts of time, often required by schools, is not practical with transaction. Transaction teaching goes "deep" into a topic, leaving less time for a superficial introduction to large quantities of information. Transaction is often misunderstood and discouraged by traditional administrators.

TRANSFORMATION

Transmission and transaction are not enough, particularly in the effort to foster justice, equality, and equity. Transformation is needed. Transformation is transaction with a purpose, and that purpose is to make a difference in the world. Transformation is defined as "teaching students to care and make a difference in the world while simultaneously trying to make a difference in the world" (Aldridge, Manning, Christensen, & Strevy, 2007, p. 27). Connie North (2008) and other scholars argue that "education for social change requires that students and teachers actively transform social injustices, not just study them. An emphasis on action in social justice education, then, challenges the notion that education is limited to developing knowledge, academic or otherwise" (p. 1190).

The term "transformation" is controversial because nobody "owns" transformation. An Internet search for "transformation" results in all types of definitions, political beliefs, religious affiliations, and ideologies. Sometimes transformation is associated with the Far Right and religious transformation. Others have used the term to refer to radical political ideas and new-age beliefs. However, our conceptions of transformation are associated with social justice. When educators and students work together to seek equality and access for everyone, they are working for social justice (Edelsky, 1999).

Transformation starts with the teacher. Teachers cannot easily incorporate transformation into classroom practices if they have not worked toward transformation. In other words, "a transformative teacher then works to make a profound and positive difference in her students' lives. The teacher consciously works to open her young students to having caring spirits and provides concrete experiences in promoting social justice" (Christensen & Aldridge, 2013, p. 78).

To that end, transformative teachers must carefully consider the context in which they teach. Teachers in rural Mississippi teach in a context that has vastly different notions of transformation than those in Seattle. While working to help students transform their school, neighborhood, or community, teachers attend to the needs, issues, values, and beliefs of those with whom they work (Kirylo, 2016b; Meier, 1995). The following is an example as to why an understanding of and sensitivity to the context is salient in determining transformational learning.

A teacher of a multiage classroom in rural Oregon works diligently to teach transformatively and involve her students in making a difference in their community. Conservationists are quite concerned in this area of Oregon with "saving the owls." However, all of the students' parents or family members in her classroom are involved in some way in the lumber business. Many of them are angry with the conservationists because conservation efforts in their community seek to limit the amount of timber that is cut, limiting the income of the families that support her students. The teacher is very interested in "saving the owls" but knows that a project that addresses this will not get the support from families and communities. Other projects are jointly chosen by the teacher and students with the support and participation of families. For example, the students adopted senior adults in a nearby nursing home. They visited them, went on outings with them, and presented plays to them among other things. They studied nursing home standards and considered ways to improve the lives of the residents. This project was successful because all stakeholders bought into it. Should the teacher never discuss "save the owls?" As with all transformation, the teacher is a reflective decision maker. She must decide what to do. However, "save the owls" would never be the first transformative study because of the controversy it would cause. Teachers at all levels wrestle with similar issues throughout their professional careers.

As in this example, students are asked to take an active role in the development of a transformative curriculum. Students are encouraged to suggest ways to make a difference in their school, neighborhood, or community, often based on the topics promoted through the traditional curriculum. For example, if students are studying recycling, they are asked to think of ways to promote and implement recycling efforts in the school and community. Transformative projects develop from the suggestions of the students (Aldridge & Goldman, 2007; Christensen & Aldridge, 2013).

The benefits of transformation can be enormous. Students work together for the good of the school, the neighborhood, the community, and the world. They can develop dispositions such as problem solving, negotiating strategies, and a transformational attitude toward learning and life. Multiple viewpoints are explored as well as issues and problems that may arise, leading students and teachers to continually evaluate and reevaluate what transformation means.

The notion of transformation, of course, does not come without challenges that sometimes become drawbacks. That is, we must continually ask, "Whose transformation is it, anyway?" (Christensen & Aldridge, 2013, p. 80). And at times there is a problem with the imposition of well-intentioned but impractical or harmful ideas; unintentional consequences can happen. Still, transformation is worth the effort. New directions and turning points in teacher education should always be concerned with the question "What type of world do we want for our students and ourselves?"

In the final analysis, transformative learning can be the result of a synergistic affect among teacher education, public schools, community, and indeed, around the globe, with the only limitation being that of the imagination.

• *14* •

Should We Emphasize Universal Human Development or Diversity?

*T*eacher education has long required teacher candidates to rightly take human development courses, which have had different course titles dictated by respective colleges. Usually the classes are called something like the following: child development, human development, developmental psychology, adolescent psychology, or child development and family relations. Through the late 20th century, the textbooks used in these classes usually began with a short history of child development and moved quickly into theories of development.

These theories were constructed by "dead white men," most of whom never taught children. Their ideas reflected their context and countries, but they were presented as gospel and rarely questioned (Aldridge, 1996). Teacher candidates had to hurriedly memorize the list of ages and stages of several theorists (e.g., Gesell, Piaget, Freud, Erikson, and Vygotsky) and learn the terminology of others who did not propose stages (e.g., Skinner, Bandura, and Bronfenbrenner), usually without thinking about them, so they could move on to the next chapter, probably on biology or prenatal development (Aldridge, Sexton, Goldman, Booker, & Werner, 1997). The question we ask is, should we be using human development theories to develop curricula when numerous problems and issues concerning them have been identified?

Many of the same theories of development are still popular in human development texts of the 21st century (Rathus, 2013; Santrock, 2014; Sigelman & Rider, 2018). The problems with applying human development theories such as behaviorism (Skinner, Bijou, and others), constructivism (Piaget, Kamii, and others), and the cultural historical approach of Vygotsky to educational practice are many. Five of the most prominent reasons for this are as follows: (1) They tend to blame the family, especially the mother, for

79

difficulties that arise in a child's development. (2) They tend to favor middle-class conceptions of child development. (3) They often ignore the context of development. (4) They promote Eurocentric values such as autonomy and independence. (5) And they have been used to prescribe instruction.

BLAMING THE FAMILY

Freud's (1935) psychoanalytic theory was used to analyze behavior disorders from the 1920s through the 1940s. As Hinshaw (1994) puts it, "Behavior problems displayed by children were viewed as symbolic manifestations of unresolved conflict, often emanating from early caregiver-child interactions" (p. 10). Other theorists blamed the home environment as well.

Gesell (1950) reported that low-income "households still use methods of harsh discipline. . . . Misguided and crude forms of child management are so widespread as to constitute a public health problem, a task of preventive mental hygiene" (p. 310). These theories totally ignore the social and political structures in which the child and family are embedded and rely on middle-class values and constructions as universal norms for child development (Burman, 2008).

MIDDLE-CLASS BIAS

Piaget's theory is often used to promote a child-centered approach to pedagogical practice, advocating "a naturalised, individualised model of childhood which confirms social privileges and pathologises those who are already socially disadvantaged" (Burman, 2008, pp. 261–262). The ideas and discourse proposed by these mentioned (and other) "dead white men" can lead to social regulation. In fact, Gesell proposed the medical supervision of low-income children and the necessity of parent education (Gesell, 1950). Thus, education becomes "the route to intervene in and reform family life" (Burman, 2008, p. 271).

DEVELOPMENT WITHOUT CONTEXT

Piaget, Freud, Erikson, and other theorists believed in universal stages of child development while ignoring the contexts within which individuals develop (Aldridge, 1996; Aldridge & Goldman, 2007; Burman, 2008). In interviews with Jean-Claude Bringuier, Jean Piaget discusses his stages. Bringuier asked Piaget if all children go through the same stages in the same order. Piaget responded, "Yes, of course. . . . Children in Martinique are in the French school system. . . . They do get through, but in my studies of operation and conversations they are four years behind" (Bringuier, 1980, p. 34).

When Bringuier asked Piaget why this was, Piaget explained, "Their society, which is lazy" (Bringuier, 1980, p. 34). Piaget does not mention that most of these children descended from slaves and did not intentionally adopt the French system. It was imposed on them. In other words, "he does not consider that their ways of thinking and operating may be different from his white, upper middle-class way of thinking. Very few texts adequately discuss this when discussing Piaget's universal, invariant stages" (Aldridge & Goldman, 2007, p. 101).

AUTONOMY AND INDEPENDENCE

Piaget also believed autonomy was the aim of education, and applications of his theory have promoted this (Kamii, 2000). Yet, notions of autonomy and independence are constructed differently from family to family and from culture to culture. In many Latinx and Asian families, for example, autonomy is encouraged much later than in Eurocentric American homes.

A white kindergarten teacher complained that a mother of one of her Latinx students came to school at lunch every day to feed her daughter. She scolded the mother. The teacher told her that the goal in her classroom was autonomy and that the mother's behavior was disruptive to this practice (Aldridge & Goldman, 2007). The kindergarten teacher was unyielding because she was taught autonomy was the aim of education in college.

PRESCRIBED INSTRUCTION

Human development theories have been used as a basis for the development of curriculum for over a century. During the second half of the 20th century, curricula reflected the theories of Piaget, Vygotsky, and sometimes Bronfenbrenner (Goldman, Aldridge, & Camp, 2008). Under No Child Left Behind (NCLB) and still prevalent up to this day, the underlying theory was behaviorism. Goals, objectives, instruction, and assessment were based, whether consciously or not, on a mechanistic, behavioral paradigm. Prescribing instruction based on theories of development or learning that do not consider the multiple contexts in which students are imbedded favor white, middle-class notions of development and do not value or use the beliefs, values, and strengths of historically disenfranchised populations.

WHAT SHOULD WE DO ABOUT CULTURE?

During the early 20th century through the early 1980s, the notion of the "culturally deprived student" was popular and taught in schools of education (Olson & Larson, 1965; Riessman, 1962, 1963; Stodolsky & Lesser, 1967) and has persisted in other countries into the 21st century (Begum, 2003).

One definition of culturally deprived was "those who have not been inducted into their own culture due to the inadequate provision of such learning" (Jensen, Feuerestein, Rand, Kaniel, & Tzuriel, 1988, p. 64). What does that mean? All people are imbedded into their own culture just as we breathe in oxygen. How can people not be inducted into their own culture?

To be sure, coming from a deficit model of viewing, cultural deprivation was code for any culture that was different from the white, middle-class Anglo-Saxon culture. As Aldridge, Kilgo, and Christensen (2014) put it, "Fifty years ago, the function of education with regard to culture was assimilation" (p. 107).

Even then, assimilation was not available for all. The integration of African Americans and other disenfranchised groups was far from a reality. Fortunately, teacher educators began to realize that the term "culturally deprived" was a social construction that favored the dominant group and marginalized others. The belief that a student could be culturally deprived began to fade as new conceptions of culture developed. Over time, multiculturalism, interculturalism, and transculturalism emerged (Aldridge, Kilgo, & Bruton, 2015; Aldridge, Kilgo, & Christensen, 2014; Banks, 2014).

MULTICULTURAL EDUCATION

Multiculturalism in education has numerous definitions. Some define it as a shift in curriculum, others focus on classroom climate and interactions, and others define it in terms of institutional and systemic changes with regard to IQ and standardized testing, school structures, and more (Gorski, 2000).

Since the 1980s, a plethora of resources related to multicultural education have emerged. Early notions of multicultural education were quite primitive. Many of these were based on a "tour" or "detour" approach (Aldridge, Calhoun, & Aman, 2000). As a tour or detour approach, different cultures were studied on the side in inadequate and superficial ways. Often this centered on food, and a feast was prepared as a culminating activity, presenting various foods from different cultures. Inaccurate generalizations were applied to whole groups.

For example, in one classroom, the teacher explained that all Spanish-speaking people enjoyed eating tacos. Today there are numerous multicultural curricula that are imbedded into everyday practices, and efforts to incorporate culture naturally through interactions with others are encouraged (Banks, 2014). However, other conceptions of culture have come to the forefront in the past two decades. One of these is intercultural education.

INTERCULTURAL EDUCATION

In an attempt to clarify misconceptions and miscommunications, Portera (2011) defined many of the terms associated with diversity and culture, including *suppression, assimilation, segregation, fusion, universalism, multiculturalism, interculturalism,* and *transculturalism.* Intercultural education is defined as "a deep engagement with diverse cultures and worldviews to enrich children and the society, rather than the celebrations of differences and the coexistence of various cultural groups" (Miller & Petriwskyj, 2013, p. 253). Intercultural education "takes into consideration both opportunities and limitations, but it transcends them and builds up a new synthesis, with improved chances of dialogue, exchange and interaction" (Portera, 2011, p. 20).

Intercultural education began in Europe in the context of education and sociology (Portera, 2011). Specifically, the French sociologist Louis Porcher and his student, Martine Abdallah-Pretceille, were the first to define intercultural education (Abdallah-Pretceille, 1990). Since the 1990s, intercultural education has developed rapidly throughout Europe and Australia (Clifford, 2011; Gundara, 2011; Lasonen, 2011; Miller & Petriwskyj, 2013).

However, in the United States, *multiculturalism* has been the preferred term for professional practices regarding diverse populations (Aldridge, Kilgo, & Christensen, 2014; Kirylo, 2017). Some of the beliefs and practices of European intercultural education have permeated multicultural education in the United States and Canada; however, the term *intercultural education* has been slow to enter the North American lexicon (Grant & Brueck, 2011).

Still, the definitions and expressed goals of intercultural education and multicultural education are different (Portera, 2011). Perhaps the biggest difference between intercultural education and multicultural education is the emphasis on deep and sustained engagement over time among diverse participants (Aldridge, Kilgo, & Bruton, 2015).

Just as multicultural education was criticized for its limitations, intercultural education has developed critics as well. Gorski (2008) explains, "Despite unquestionably good intentions on the part of most people who call themselves intercultural educators, most intercultural education practice supports, rather than challenges dominant hegemony, prevailing social hierarchies, and inequitable distributions of power and privilege" (p. 515). Something beyond multicultural an intercultural education is needed. Could that be transcultural education?

TRANSCULTURAL EDUCATION

The use of the term *transcultural education* has been used sparingly in the educational literature. Until recently a definitive definition of transcultural education was not proposed (Aldridge, Kilgo, & Christensen, 2014). Like intercultural education, it has been used primarily in Europe, and even then, it was used to refer to specific types of education such as nursing education, Christian education, and global education (Cook, Sheerin, Bancel, & Rodrigues Gomes, 2012; Hill, 1992; Wulf, 2010).

In fact, Aldridge, Kilgo, and Christensen (2014) did not specifically define *transcultural education* but instead asked the question "What is transcultural education?" and discussed the possibilities as to what the *trans-* in transcultural education means. To begin with, they used *culture* or *culturing* as a verb instead of a noun because "culture as a noun implies a fixed entity; however, culture is fluid. Acculturation is something done to our students and to us. If we refer to culturing, then we are discussing actions within and between individuals and groups of people" (p. 108). They discuss five possibilities as to what the *trans-* means in transcultural. Two of these are important to our discussions here. These include *transferential culturing* and *transcendent culturing*.

Transferential culturing refers to "code switching" when interacting with different groups or individuals. Different individuals, groups, and cultures have disparate interaction styles. Further, we navigate among, between, and within various cultures every day. When teachers interact with students, they have a different interaction style than with their principal, partner, best friend, or the clerk at the grocery store. In each case, they use different language and accommodate their interactions depending on whom they are speaking with. Problems arise when the interaction style of another individual, group, or culture is not understood (Lynch & Hanson, 2011). Transferential culturing is defined as "operating, interacting, or using the dominant culture's expectations. Dominant in this case means the dominant for a specific group in which others are a minority" (Aldridge, Kilgo, & Christensen, 2014, p. 109).

For example, if you eat with certain Arabic families, you are expected to sit on the floor and eat with your hands. If you dine with some Brazilians, you would be expected to always use a utensil, even with a pizza, and if you go to some traditional Chinese homes, chopsticks are provided for use.

While transferential culturing with a focus on code switching is a possibility for transcultural education, transferential culturing is misleading because it assumes that every culture is a monoculture, which often stereotypes and stifles authentic interactions. "Culture does not designate a self-contained, uniquely definable ensemble of practices, values, symbolizations and imaginations. The borders between cultures are dynamic and change according to context. They are permeable" (Wulf, 2010, p. 34).

Transcendent culturing is interacting with others through transcending or overcoming cultural barriers that limit human interaction. This involves deconstructing traditional cultural labels with a movement toward building communities based on uniquely individual identities that contribute and benefit from the ever-changing group dynamics and structures. Developing a transcultural curriculum that is based on transcendence opens the door to seven possibilities. Each will be described here.

Transcendent culturing accommodates "hybrid cultures." A hybrid culture is defined as "any cultural context, especially within and between families, which synthesizes more than one culture with another producing a synergistic effect" (Aldridge, Kilgo, & Christensen, 2014, p. 113). In the 1950s and 1960s, *Father Knows Best* and *Leave It to Beaver* were television shows that extolled the benefits of the Anglo-Saxon middle-class traditional family. In the 21st century, other types of families are portrayed, including hybrid families such as in *Modern Family* or *Black-ish* (Aldridge, Kilgo, & Bruton, 2016). The following vignette portrays an example of a hybrid family whose children attend public schools.

Selena, from Venezuela, has lived in Denver most of her life since her family immigrated when she was a child. Selena and her family are devout Catholics. When Selena was in her 20s, she sought to marry a good Catholic Latino man. This never happened, and in her 30s she fell in love with Pawi, an immigrant from Malaysia. Pawi and his family are devout Muslims. Today, Selena and Pawi have two children, Daniela and Aldi, who attend the public schools of Denver. Selena takes the children to church on Sundays, and Pawi takes them to the mosque on Fridays. Both children are in after-school Arabic classes so they will learn to read the Quran. Daniela and Aldi are also being prepared for confirmation in the Catholic Church. Neither child speaks Spanish or Malay.

If this hybrid family is addressed at all in classrooms, it would most likely be described as Latinx, South American, Malaysian, or Southeast Asian.

Daniela and Aldi never see themselves in children's books or class discussions. Why do educators not see the fluidity and hybrid nature of culture in the 21st century?

Both multicultural and intercultural education advocates have begun to recognize the need to see culture through a different lens. However, when trying to address the deficiencies of how culture is taught, they both dedicated far more attention to the differences between and among cultures than they have to the intracultural variability within each child in the classroom. This intracultural variability can be seen *within* Daniela and Aldi in the vignette presented here. Children from a Venezuelan Malaysian American background who participates in two religions have unique cultural variations *within*, not just *between*, themselves and others. Further, most students today will find cultural conflict within themselves as well as between themselves and others. For example, a high school student raised in a Mormon household who identifies as a lesbian will need support in dealing with her internal cultural milieu.

We are not just products of our culture but also producers (Vygotsky, 1978). A transculturalist's job is to be the producer of something new, not just maintaining the status quo as a product of culture. Multicultural and intercultural education focus more on how we are products of culture and not enough on how we are producers of culture. Transculturalists should take the lead in investigating how we, as teachers and students, are producers of culture—of something new.

Transcultural educators are called to transcend culture in order to create something new and innovative. This is what Joseph Campbell referred to as the "call to adventure" (Campbell, 2008, p. 48). This call "signifies that destiny has summoned the hero and transferred his spiritual center of gravity from within the pale of his society to a zone unknown" (p. 48). Campbell believed that the hero must go into the world to find his or her own way, but also has a moral obligation to bring something back to society and culture as a whole. Creation springs "from insights, sentiments, thoughts, and visions of an adequate individual, loyal to his own experience of value" (Campbell, 1968, pp. 6–7).

Transcultural education can also help in addressing tribalism. While "shiny objects" are sources of distraction for those teaching and learning about human development, as described in an earlier section of this chapter, tribalism is the major obstacle in understanding cultures and interacting with others. Those who do not believe this should consider the polarized "tribal warfare" that manifested itself during the presidency of Donald Trump.

Wilson (2014) describes how a human is part of a tribe, just as ants or bees. Our language, thoughts, religion, and views of the world are shaped by the tribes in which we are members. Identification with a tribe is part of human existence, but when social and educational changes occur, the shadow side of tribalism raises its ugly head. For decades, the pendulum has swung from one "tribal position" to another.

Educators have tried to stop the pendulum swing for decades (Jalongo, 1999). We suggest breaking the pendulum for good. This cannot be done until educators recognize the pendulum swing follows the dictates of enantiodromia. "Enantiodromia is a psychological 'law' first outlined by Heraclitus and meaning that sooner or later everything turns into its opposite" (Samuels, Shorter, & Plaut, 1986, p. 53). The teaching of culture has done just that. "With the assimilationists, all familial and cultural practices that were not part of the dominant culture were considered worthless, inferior, or savage. As multiculturalism and interculturalism developed, the opposite problem transpired" (Aldridge, Kilgo, & Christensen, 2014, p. 114). This leads us to the next point.

How far should we go in honoring and respecting culture? Consider the following questions:

1. Nazi Germany was a culture. Are we to embrace all cultures with open arms and not question their abominable practices?
2. A father from another country comes to school for a parent/teacher conference. He tells the female teacher of his son that he does not speak to women about his children's education. Is she expected to hurriedly leave the room and find a man in the school to mediate? What if there are no men in that school? What if this had been a white father telling an African American teacher that he did not talk to Black people about his child's education? We have witnessed education faculty members encouraging the female teacher to accommodate the father from another country and his culture. Really?
3. We discuss apartheid in South Africa and how the United States placed sanctions on that country during that period. Yet in other parts of Africa they still practice female genital mutilation and child labor, and sentence gay men to death and the United States has not placed sanctions. In fact, it has provided aid to the countries. Other nations deny education to females and allow them to be sold into prostitution and slavery? Do we not question these cultural practices that are often norms?

Finally, transcultural education challenges us to question the purpose of education that maintains the status quo, suggesting that being passive and conforming and blind obedience is not an option if we aim to progressively move forward (Chomsky, 2012).

• 15 •

The Question of Online Delivery Systems in Teacher Education

"*W*ould you like to earn your master's degree in your bathrobe? Well, we have just the program for you! Jumbo University has more than 20 online programs in education at the undergraduate and graduate levels. Enroll today!" Believe it or not, we have seen advertisements that were as ridiculous as this one.

Until the beginning of the 21st century, the vast majority of teacher education programs delivered instruction in some type of face-to-face setting. For the past 15 years, however, a large number of teacher education programs have begun to deliver instruction online. Numerous formats and platforms have been used by faculties, but most can be divided into three categories: (1) total in-class instruction, (2) total online instruction, and (3) blended instruction. The following examples are of actual faculty members who represent one of these methods of delivery. Each instructor was interviewed and asked to describe his or her choices and experiences.

TOTAL IN-CLASS INSTRUCTION

The following instructor has taught for more than 30 years at three different Research 1 universities. He has never taught online and does not plan to do so. He explains,

> The program in which I teach has interdisciplinary course work for graduate students representing multiple disciplines who enroll in classes together to learn to work as members of teams. Students who graduate from this program must have skills to work effectively with professionals from other disciplines.

Traditional on-ground instruction is required for them to have opportunities to develop the skills needed to work as members of teams (e.g., joint problem solving, conflict resolution, communication, and collaboration).

The strengths of on-ground courses provide opportunities for both students and teachers. Students and teacher have an opportunity to get to know one another on a personal level. Students learn from each other in a number of ways. For example, students are able to receive honest and immediate feedback from other students. Faculty members gain a greater understanding of student performance.

Moreover, they are able to observe firsthand who is committed from attendance, interaction, and contributions to class projects and discussions. Faculty members are also able to observe and receive feedback from the students to know if they are understanding and applying the information and material. Faculty members cannot only readily determine the dispositions of students but also observe the interactions of students. A face-to-face format allows for team-based, relationship-oriented skills to be taught, modeled, practiced, applied, and assessed.

However, there are weaknesses to only on-ground courses. On-ground courses are not as convenient for students with full or erratic schedules. Also, some students' personalities and personal learning styles and preferences may fit better with online courses. While traditional courses may preserve the quality of the content and skills acquired in courses, they may have fewer students enrolled than online courses.

There are things that need to be changed about on-ground courses. The main thing that would be helpful to change with traditional on-ground courses is the degree of rigidity often associated with traditional formats. For example, college and university schedules are often rigid (e.g., start time and number of class meetings). Another change would be to make greater use of technology so that it is more convenient for students. Blended formats often make good use of both types of classes.

TOTAL ONLINE INSTRUCTION

The next instructor has taught for more than 20 years in higher education at four separate institutions; her current university has a Research 1 designation. She explains why she is teaching completely online without any on-ground instruction.

> I was hired to teach for the expressed purpose of teaching online graduate education courses. So, my designation as an online instructor came with the "job description." Of course, most, if not all, mainstream universities have online classes, both at the undergraduate and graduate level.
>
> I completely understand this trajectory as we are more and more immersed in this "age of technology" and especially for the younger gen-

eration; they are growing up using this medium in multiple forms and fashions. But, perhaps more importantly, if mainstream universities do not offer online type classes, droves of potential students will attend the University of Phoenix–type settings. That is not a good thing.

So, a strength, if you will, of online delivery systems at mainstream universities is simply a response to the signs of the times, responding to the "market." In addition, another strength is that, especially for students who live in rural areas, live far away from university settings, or live in high-density urban areas with heavy traffic, or for those who have little or no transportation, online venues open up opportunities.

Also, more and more students are working, raising families, where their time is stretched too thin. An online venue, which cuts out travel time, allows for flexibility and can be good for those students.

Finally, for some students, working through an online venue frees them to be more authentic in their online interaction with others as opposed to being in class face-to-face where for whatever reason they may be shy, hesitant, or resistant to participate in class.

There are, of course, weaknesses of totally online instruction. Especially for the field of education, where the work is interacting with people (e.g., students, colleagues, and parents), it is extremely difficult in an online venue to "assess" a student's disposition, who he or she is as a person, and what kind of teacher he or she will potentially be.

To put it another way, if a student were to ask me to write a letter of recommendation for a potential job, I would have difficulty because I would have never met the person (only through online). As a teacher educator, it is important to meet and interact with teacher candidates.

Moreover, through the online medium, as a teacher educator, I am not really able to authentically observe how students interact with one another in person. There are some online forums where students can interact electronically, in face-to-face-type time, but for me that is not the same as being in the same room regularly with others to observe that dynamic.

Teaching completely online is difficult. In a sense, I need to further change to keep up with the times and better inform myself how to better and more effectively use online instruction. Particularly for undergraduates, I would suggest that we monitor and be very careful to not over-offer online classes. It is important that teacher educators meet and spend time in person with teacher candidates.

BLENDED INSTRUCTION

The third instructor has taught for 32 years, full time, at four universities, and eight years as an adjunct; his current university has a research 1 designation.

He discusses the preferences and concerns about teaching in class, online, and blended courses.

> I have taught in-class, blended, and online classes. After teaching in public schools for several years, I began teaching at a small state university in the rural area of a southern state. At that time, I had no choice but to teach in class since the Internet had not yet been created. However, the College of Education did have what I would call a "Stone Age" version of distance education. Graduate courses were often taught in rural communities anywhere from 35 to 150 miles from campus.
>
> As a new faculty member, I was assigned several of these courses. These classes met from 6:00 to 10:00 p.m. once a week at night because the university had 10-week sessions on the quarter system. I would often have to teach on campus the next day at 9:00 a.m. This was a grueling schedule because I lived 60 miles from the university and all of the off-campus courses were in the other direction of where I lived from the university.
>
> I still prefer to teach on campus, in face-to-face meetings with the students, but over time I began to prefer a blended format depending on the nature of the course I taught. I found the blended format to be the best of both worlds. In the blended courses I have taught, the class has met four times a semester, with specific assignments to be turned in online and an electronic discussion board that has been used with what I hope are well-designed assignments that fit this format.
>
> And then there is the totally online format. Forgive my vernacular, but as my grandmother would have said, "Lord, help us all!" I found this form of instruction to be the most overwhelming, particularly the first time I attempted it. I have to admit, I am not technologically oriented in my daily life. I do not have a Facebook, Twitter, or Snapchat account and don't plan on getting them. You can imagine how overwhelmed I was the first time I taught totally online.
>
> The College of Education had a technology coordinator who was supposed to help faculty members set up their online classes. He gave me five minutes of instruction. He basically said, "Go in and put the stuff online." So I was left to fend for myself. Over time there have been several different platforms that have been used for online instruction at my university. I do not use them as they were designed.
>
> For example, rather than using a Dropbox, I have students submit all assignments to an e-mail account that I established specifically for the class. I also have to say that, for me, totally online instruction is, by far, the most difficult teaching I have ever done. First of all, I personally chose to develop assignments in which the students would have extreme difficulty cheating. Usually, the assignments involve applications of what students have studied.
>
> I also develop my own lectures but change them over time, of course, to fit the context. For example, there was a devastating tornado in the area

one year, and my application assignments for the child psychology class I taught had to reflect what they would do related to the recent tornado, based on material we had discussed online and that they had studied. The other thing that was a major challenge at first was my perceived need of the students for me to be online 24 hours a day at their beck and call. I had to learn how to establish boundaries and parameters to deal with this.

Overall, depending on the course, I prefer blended classes. They are the best of both worlds and also the best use of my time and hopefully the students' time.

What these three very real examples obviously tell us is that there are advantages and disadvantages to each of the three types of delivery systems we described (in class, online, and blended). Methods courses for undergraduate students should have a strong in-class component, as well as observation, participation, and practicum experiences that are face-to-face. In the earliest stages of teacher education course work, students need this interaction, as they will most likely be delivering most of their instruction in public schools face-to-face.

Students who have completed an initial teacher certification program and are continuing their education at the graduate level may benefit from a blended or totally online program. This is true not only in education but also in related professions such as occupational therapy and physical therapy. These programs are predominantly in-class programs for their initial education at the master's level. However, students continuing at the doctoral level may attend a blended or totally online program.

Blended and online programs are still in their infancy, and more research needs to be conducted on their effectiveness in teacher education programs. Research studies need to be conducted not only on their efficacy but also on the college instructors' perceptions and preferences. Some professors are better suited to in-class meetings, while others have a propensity for online instruction.

V

TEACHER EDUCATION AND MOVING FORWARD

• 16 •

Realize the Distraction in Order to Move Forward

In a provocative piece titled "Last Stand for Teacher Education," Fischetti (2013) shares a scene from a 2012 motion picture, *Man on a Ledge*, narrating that the main character is stubbornly standing outside on a ledge threatening to jump from the top of a high-rise building. "His actions, however, are a ruse, a purposeful distraction. His brother is attempting to rob a diamond from a vault just a few blocks away and the man on the ledge is his accomplice. His role is to keep the police at bay by keeping law enforcement personnel resources focused on the ledge—letting their guard down to the real crime that is being committed" (p. 41).

Valerie Strauss is a well-informed education writer for the *Washington Post*, and her January 13, 2014, article is titled "Is Teacher Education a Disaster?"[1] In this feature, Strauss gives way to the work of Mike Rose, a professor at the UCLA Graduate School of Education.[2] Worthy of citing a passage in its entirety, Rose states,

> College and university-based teacher education programs vary considerably by size, region, student body, nature and focus of curriculum, talent of instructional staff, status within home institution, balance of course work and practice, relation with local district, and more. Some are excellent, some are good and experimenting with ways to get better, some are weak in some respects but decent in others, some are marginal and poorly run. The language of the current criticism of teacher ed, at least the most public language, doesn't allow for this variability. Nor does the dismissive rhetorical stance of the most vocal critics, the tone and attitude running through their language. The bottom-line message: Teacher education is a disaster. (para. 1)

As we learned in the chapters in parts 3 and 4 of this text, teacher education itself not only has a rocky or unsteady history but also appears to be perpetually negotiating its identity within its own collective political bubble, uniquely played out at individual university-based teacher education sites. In other words, Rose, of course, is correct that on multiple levels there is variability among teacher education programs across the country, as there is with any large enterprise.

The problem and to reiterate, as he makes clear, is that the current chatter that dominates the analysis of teacher education is one that does not allow for that variability. In other words, this chatter is one—as was underscored in part 2 of this text—in which a neoliberal-led perspective dominates the effort to ultimately eliminate traditional teacher education programs. In short, the hijacking of the teacher education narrative is one that looks to convince the general public and shape political sway that teacher education is a collective disaster.

Yet the myopic notion of teacher education being a collective disaster is a distraction as with the man on the ledge, while the real "crime" that is being committed is the systematic undermining of what it means, what it takes, and what is necessary to be a professional educator. Not only that, the unmitigated rhetoric, with its "sweeping language of failure, narrows the understanding we have of a problem and leads to solutions that create problems of their own" (Rose, 2014, para. 2).

To be clear, while the distractive apparatus undermining teacher education has been in play for years, we are not suggesting that traditional teacher education programs do not have room for improvement or are above criticism. On the contrary, the nature of the individual teacher to the operation of teacher education institutions themselves ought to be always in the process of tweaking, to be better and to improve. Rose indeed is correct to point out the variability among teacher education institutions across the country. And of course within that variability some are marginal and poorly run, while still others are doing an exemplary job (Darling-Hammond, 2006).

The way toward improvement, toward addressing the negative variability, is not one that ought to be directed by castigating the entire enterprise, to only move into a "solution" that is problematic in itself as Rose suggests. And while there must be an astute awareness of the involved dynamics and the generalizations that are being asserted, we must not lose focus by staying in the weeds with the rhythm of that distraction. In other words, as Fischetti (2013) exhorts, "while teacher educators should necessarily be wise, strategic, and even challenge the multiple forces that are attempting to undermine the relevance of teacher education, they must not allow those forces to distract them from their core mission" (p. 41).

In other words, teacher education as an entity—uniquely manifested at teacher programs across the country—must be focused on who they are as a profession, looking to always affirm, celebrate, and make known the good things they are doing but also being thoughtful, reflective, and forward-thinking on where they can improve. Of course, working toward that end is not quite that simple.

PUBLIC FICKLENESS

The challenge, as has been in the history of teacher education and the teaching profession in general, is that the profession as a whole has struggled with its own identity, largely dictated by a fickle public

- that seemingly wants their K–12 schools staffed with well-prepared quality teachers yet is willing to accept microwaved teacher preparation programs;
- that is willing to accept noncertified teachers and nonqualified superintendents at the district and state levels;
- that seemingly desires teachers to be professionals but is skittish about competitive salaries as compared to other high-profile professions; and
- that seemingly wants teachers to be insightful, energetic critical thinkers but wants them to know their place and adhere to oppressive top-down control, is quick to blame them for societal ills, and overall is noncommittal when it comes to fostering the professionalization of teaching.

Indeed, this fickleness places schoolteachers in the precarious position where they are expected to be present but not to have a voice, and where they are especially needed but not generously rewarded and are expected to be at "the beck and call of the public" (Herbst, 1989, p. 3). For this and other reasons Hargreaves and Lo (2000) characterize teaching as a profession that is uniquely paradoxical:

> Teaching is . . . charged with the formidable task of creating the human skills and capacities that will enable societies to survive and succeed in the age of information. . . . At the same time, public expenditure, public welfare and public education are among the first expendable casualties of the slimmed-down state that informational societies and their economies seem to require. Just when the very most is expected of them, teachers appear to be given less support, less respect, and less opportunity to be creative, flexible and innovative than before. (pp. 1–2)

In the end, therefore, in a society in which income is equated with social worth, and in which an excellent education, autonomy, a code of ethics, and authority is tied to being a professional, it should be no surprise that teachers have historically not been viewed as professionals (Herbst, 1989). In addition, the feminized status of teaching in the United States is "the reason that teaching has not risen to the level of full-fledged profession such as medicine and law" (Santoro, 2018, p. 26).

Yet we know that one of the most important determiners that affects student learning and achievement gains is contingent upon the degree of the quality of the teacher. In fact, the likelihood of this degree of student success is highly magnified for those students who are taught by a high-quality teacher over successive years as opposed to those students who are assigned to ineffective teachers who will have a detrimental effect on student learning for successive years (Darling-Hammond, 2006).

And still further, according to a 2014 Phi Delta Kappa (PDK) Gallup poll and other polls that indicate similar sentiments, the American public believes the quality of teachers is extremely important, supporting the idea of more rigorous entrance requirements, and clearly wants a national board certification component (Bushaw, 2014). The problem, however, is that the paradoxical place that the teaching profession continues to find itself in is that the public desire is at odds with public commitment, which in the end works to minimize the teaching profession and to dismantle the public square. What is needed, as will be explored in the following chapter, is what we are characterizing as a "Flexner-like moment."

NOTES

1. The notion of Strauss being a well-informed education writer is no small matter. Many education writers from around the country are either ill informed or not informed when it comes to the complex nature inherent in education, often resulting in a distorted reporting of education happenings. Indeed, as Hancock (2005) argues, the newspaper media, particularly those who conduct school reporting, should become more intimately informed regarding the complexities of schooling. Being more informed would greatly assist them in probing more deeply, asking important questions, and reporting more carefully regarding the affairs of education. Put another way and in short, "Reporters have an obligation to notice when they are being taken for a ride and they should refuse to go along" (Lakoff, 2004, p. 50).

2. Rose's January 13, 2014, piece was part 3 of a series on teacher education that Strauss highlighted in the *Washington Post*. Part 1 is titled "Why Educating the Educators Is Complex" (see Strauss, 2013a). Part 2 is titled "What's Right—and Very Wrong—with the Teacher Education Debate" (see Strauss, 2013b).

• *17* •

In Need of a "Flexner-Like" Moment in Teacher Education

In the annals of medical education history in the United States and Canada, Abraham Flexner's name emerges as one of the most important figures, particularly with respect to the release of his 1910 report entitled *Medical Education in the United States and Canada*, or what is simply known as the "Flexner Report." In contrast to how the practice of medicine was viewed in Europe as a professional calling, the United States at the time of the report saw the practice of medicine as a trade (Lear, 1965).

And as a point of clarification, *Merriam-Webster* (2012) defines *trade* as an occupation, business, or industry; hence a tradesperson learns a skill to become, for example, a carpenter, plumber, or electrician. And a *profession* is defined as a calling, often requiring long and intensive academic preparation; hence a profession requires university work, often postgraduate work, as for doctors, attorneys, teachers, and journalists. However, the lines are often blurred when it comes to characterizing what occupation is considered professional. That is, people can obviously be viewed as a professional in their craft, whether carpenters, plumbers, lawyers, or teachers. The difference underscored here, however, is that a tradesperson's training generally does not require enrollment in a university, whereas a profession requires extensive university work.

In his report, Flexner found significant problems with the operations of the proprietary school infrastructure that dominated medical training. This model was a for-profit enterprise in which success was dictated by financial gain; consequently, entrance requirements were woeful (even admitting applicants without a high school degree), training was didactic with no clinical study, and a medical degree was gained within 32 weeks (Ludmerer, 2010; Flexner, 1910).

Clearly, the medical field as a professional arena of endeavor was not critically lifted up; rather, it was undermined by the personal interests and profits of the private owners of the schools. As a result of Flexner's examination of the 155 medical schools in the United States and Canada, he recommended not only that the number of schools be sizably reduced to 31 but also that medical schooling should be linked to universities, with Johns Hopkins University School of Medicine serving as a model (Ludmerer, 2010; Flexner, 1910).

In that light, Flexner went on to recommend that entrance requirements be rigorous and that medical schools be well funded in order to maintain high quality, viewing them as an entity to serve the public good. As Ludmerer (2010) puts it, Flexner "defined medical schools as public trusts—that is, as public service corporations to be run for the benefit of society, not private businesses to be operated for the profit of their stakeholders" (p. 195).

While Flexner's report was only stating the obvious that many in the medical field already knew and were working to change, his report grabbed public attention, giving rise to the overhaul of medical education. Proprietary schools were scrapped, medical training and its association with universities and hospitals became standard, monies were raised, better facilities were built, clinical work became integral, and full-time research faculties came on board, all of which extraordinarily transformed medical education as we contemporarily know it. It is ironic that the individual who is credited with dramatically changing the course of medical education in the United States and Canada was not only a former secondary school teacher but also influenced by John Dewey and the progressive education movement (Ludmerer, 2010).

The ironies, of course, have not gone unnoticed as to how the medical profession was viewed in the early 1900s and what the teaching profession continues to struggle with today:

- Whereas Flexner denounced the commercialism (i.e., proprietary schools driven by profit) of medical education as the antithesis to professionalism (Hafferty & Castellani, 2010), the current practice of "fast-track" routes toward teacher certification is equally antithetical to professionalism. Moreover, many teach without certification, some work toward it on the job, and some never attain it.
- Whereas Flexner recommended rigorous entrance requirements and strengthening medical education, many have been active in questioning the importance of teacher education programs, even looking toward abolishing them.

- Whereas Flexner rejected the idea that one could learn to be an MD by simply "following another doctor around in a buggy," many see learning the art and science of teaching as a process that simply follows a teacher around in that same buggy.[1]
- Whereas Flexner linked medical education and professionalism to public service and the social good (Hafferty & Castellani, 2010), public education and public school teachers are under assault by powerful forces fostering the privatization of education.
- Whereas Flexner saw society as integral in underwriting the cost for candidates to study to be a physician (Hafferty & Castellani, 2010), universities today are tuition-driven enterprises, affecting the incursion of student loan debt, even more exacerbated for teacher candidates who are in a field that does not pay well upon graduation.
- Whereas Flexner, a former secondary school teacher, has his stamp of work in professionalizing the medical profession, uplifting its esteem in multiple ways, it appears that the teaching profession is still waiting for that eureka moment in which there is no doubt it is more than a trade but is rather a profession.

Finally, whereby John Dewey's influence on Flexner was evident even while Flexner promoted the critical importance of the science of medical education, Dewey was cast to the side by Edward L. Thorndike in comprehending Dewey's conception of the science of education. Dewey and Thorndike were contemporaries, both viewing education as a science. However, whereas Thorndike was a behaviorist who argued that the science of education makes its relevance when it can be precisely measured,[2] Dewey, who was a pragmatist and progressive, viewed the science of education as one that was linked to sociology, philosophy, and psychology (i.e., a social science; Kirylo, 2016b; Lagemann, 2000).

While on one hand Dewey—through Flexner's work—had an influence on medical education, launching its path toward transformative change, Thorndike, on the other hand—had no use for Dewey—greatly influencing the direction of K–12 education and launching the path toward the standardization movement and, by extension, the persistence of viewing teaching more as a trade than a profession.

In other words, Thorndike patriarchally saw women in particular aptly filling their role as teachers, viewing teaching as more of a functionary or technical endeavor, and thought men were more gifted for administrative positions and leadership roles.[3] In short, Thorndike thought "teachers should come to understand their subordinate place in the educational hierarchy" (Lagemann, 2000, p. 60).[4]

RECEIVING TRAINING IS DIFFERENT FROM RECEIVING AN EDUCATION

Viewing teaching as a trade provokes the idea that one needs to be trained to work that trade as opposed to being educated. As mentioned in chapter 2, there is a certain association between receiving training and receiving an education, but those two concepts possess distinct differences.

In an editorial piece, Ohio State University professor Robert H. Essenhigh (2000) articulates the difference between training and educating, arguing that universities are "*not* in the business of 'training.' Their business is 'educating'" (p. 46). Essenhigh further explains the difference between the two concepts:

> It's the difference between *know how* and *know why*. It's the difference between, say, being *trained* as a pilot to fly a plane and being *educated* as an aeronautical engineer and knowing why the plane flies, and then being able to improve its design so that it will fly better. Clearly both are necessary, so this is not putting down the Know-How person; if I am flying from *here* to *there* I want to be in the plane with a trained pilot (though if the pilot knows the *Why* as well, then all the better, particularly in an emergency). The difference, also, is fundamentally that *Know How* is learning to Think Other People's Thoughts, which indeed is also the first stage in education—in contrast to learning to Think Your Own Thoughts, which is why *Know Why* is the final state of education. Indeed, both Know How and Know Why are essential at one moment or another, and they interact all the time; but at the same time, the center of gravity of education is and must be in the Know Why. . . . If a student tells me, in the middle of taking a core-required thermodynamics or fluid dynamics course, "Don't give me all that theoretical stuff; just give me the equation and tell me how to use it," then I know that the student wants to be trained, not educated. (p. 46)

If teaching is a profession on par with that of being an attorney, an aeronautical engineer, or a medical doctor, then an education must be required in which entrance requirements are rigorous and thoughtful, programs should be rooted in the "know why" with a practical understanding of the "know how," the pay should be competitive and attractive, and the profession itself should be held in high esteem.[5]

Darling-Hammond (n.d.) reasons that a profession minimally possesses three features: first, upon admittance to the profession, like the Hippocratic oath in medicine, one is above all committed to the well-being of one's clients; second, in addition to mastering a common base of knowledge, one has also mastered its application in order to well serve one's clients; and third, those in professions accept the responsibility for delineating, communicating, and compelling standards of practice in order to protect the people they are designed to serve.

Furthermore, Darling-Hammond (2006) argues that while professions such as law, medicine, or engineering each have their own set of complexities, the teaching profession may be inherently more complex, as teachers need to thoughtfully negotiate the multiple variables associated with working with a diverse student population.

So, teachers, while mindful of group needs, must consider individual needs; must be mindful of appropriate concepts related to learning, development, social, cultural, and language contexts; must be mindful of learning differences, how to engage students, and curricula and teaching challenges; and, finally, must be mindful of how to sort through the political nature of schooling in which school boards, legislators, administrators, colleagues, parents, and others are involved.

A TURNING POINT

In chapter 1, we asked the question, What is currently happening in education that demands we move toward an activist turning-point response? This text then sketched out the external forces that are at work to dismantle teacher education, and it also highlighted the internal forces at play in which teacher education grapples within itself. Indeed, both demand activist responses on our part. For the former, we must be diligent and resist, and for the latter we must affirm where we are doing well and change, tweak, or modify where needed. And whether it is in response to the former or the latter, we must all work toward that Flexner-like moment. As with what occurred in the medical profession more than a century ago, teaching must be treated as a high-esteemed, well-respected, and well-compensated profession.

This will demand commitment, as were the heroic individuals we highlighted in the first part of the text who in their unique ways responded to challenging and even difficult times related to educational policy, practices, curriculum, instruction, justice, equity, and equality. And they each made a difference turning the direction of education to a better road. Here our hope is that this text will make a difference in prompting thought and action in which teacher education turns toward the highly esteemed, well-respected, and well-compensated profession it ought to be.

NOTES

1. With respect to the "buggy" reference, Darling-Hammond (2010a) makes the following point: "As in teaching today, there were those who argued against the professionalization of medicine, including those who felt that medicine could best be learned by following another doctor around in a buggy" (p. 39).

2. Dubbed as the "father of the measurement movement," Thorndike viewed the mind as a physiological object, and his educational studies "favored precise, numerical measurements of anything and everything relevant to education—mental capacities, changes in behavior, and even the aims of education" (Lagemann, 2000, pp. 57, 59).

3. Of course, in the 21st century, the majority of teachers are women, and it is no coincidence that the teacher strikes we have been witnessing in several states come at the heels of the MeToo Movement. Whether it is the thinking of Thorndike, with palpable remnants still evident today, in more ways than one as underscored in this text, women (teachers) are simply done with the disrespect, the undermining of the profession, and the assault that virtually blames public education for everything that ails the United States. For an insightful reflection on this, see Nichols (2018).

4. It is worthwhile to remark that Thorndike never taught children, and as Lagemann (2000) notes, he thought of himself more as a psychologist than an educator. The long-term implication of the latter suggests that those immersed as educational researchers search for truth, and practitioners simply focus on application.

5. As it currently stands, however, the corporatized reform package appears to appeal to the political expediency of scores of politicians and the approval of many policy makers who often do not know much about education and for the most part simply see teaching as an act of transmission. In other words, as Darling-Hammond (n.d.) argues, we have created the idea that as long as teachers are provided with the necessary textbooks, the procedures to follow, and the tests to administer, students will magically get taught, all devoid of any importance regarding relationships and the reciprocal process in the teaching and learning endeavor. In concert with a neoliberal schema, this reductionist viewpoint of seeing teaching as an act of transmission has perpetuated a perspective that teaching is more like a trade than a profession, playing a considerable part in fostering the perception that the teaching profession is on the low-status end of the career ladder. As a natural extension, as discussed in chapter 3–5, it should be no surprise then that the concept of teacher preparation in the United States has historically been swimming upstream in an ongoing struggle to gain respect.

References

Abdallah-Pretceille, M. (1990). *Vers une pedagogie interculturelle*. Paris: INRP Sorbonne.

Aldridge, J. (1996). Evaluating and selecting human development texts. *College Student Journal, 30*(1), 90–92.

Aldridge, J., Calhoun, C., & Aman, R. (2000). 15 misconceptions about multicultural education. *ACEI Focus on Elementary, 12*, 1–6.

Aldridge, J., & Christensen, L. M. (2013). *Stealing from the mother: The marginalization of women in education and psychology from 1900–2010*. Lanham, MD: Rowman & Littlefield.

Aldridge, J., Christensen, L. M., & Emfinger, K. (2010). Epilogue: Pulling it all together. In J. D. Kirylo & A. K. Nauman (Eds.), *Curriculum development: Perspectives from around the world*. Olney, MD: Association for Childhood Education International.

Aldridge, J., Emfinger, K., & Martin, K. (2006). Curriculum frameworks, approaches, and models in early childhood education: What's the difference? *Focus on Teacher Education, 7*(2), 3–7.

Aldridge, J., & Goldman, R. (2007). *Current issues and trends in education* (2nd ed.). Boston, MA: Pearson.

Aldridge, J., Kilgo, J., & Bruton, A. K. (2015). Transforming transdisciplinary early intervention in early intervention and early childhood special education through intercultural education. *International Journal of Early Childhood Special Education, 7*(2), 340–357.

Aldridge, J., Kilgo, J., & Bruton, A. K. (2016). Beyond the Brady Bunch: Hybrid families and their evolving relationships with early childhood educators. *Childhood Education, 92*(2), 140–148.

Aldridge, J., Kilgo, J., & Christensen, L. M. (2014). Turning culture upside down: The role of transcultural education. *Social Studies Research and Practice, 9*(2), 107–119.

Aldridge, J., Kilgo, J., & Emfinger, K. (2010). The marginalization of women educators: A consequence of No Child Left Behind? *Childhood Education, 87*(1), 41–47.

Aldridge, J., Manning, M., Christensen, L., & Strevy, D. (2007). Teaching for transformation. In J. Aldridge & R. Goldman (Eds.), *Moving toward transformation: Teaching and learning in inclusive classrooms* (pp. 27–32). Birmingham, AL: Seacoast.

Aldridge, J., Sexton, D., Goldman, R., Booker, B., & Werner, M. (1997). Examining contributions of child development theories to early childhood education. *College Student Journal, 31*(4), 453–459.

Antler, J. (1987). *Lucy Sprague Mitchell: The making of a modern woman.* New Haven, CT: Yale University Press.

Anyon, J. (2005). *Radical possibilities: Public policy, urban education, and a new social movement.* New York, NY: Routledge.

Apple, M. (2000). *Official knowledge: Democratic education in a conservative age* (2nd ed.). New York, NY: Routledge.

Armstrong, F. (2002). The historical development of special education: Humanitarian rationality or "wild profusion of entangled events"? *History of Education, 31*(5), 437–456.

Banks, J. (2014). *An introduction to multicultural education* (5th ed.). Boston, MA: Pearson.

Begum, S. (2003). *Cognitive development of culturally deprived children.* New Delhi, India: Sarup & Sons.

Best, H. (1930). Educational provisions for the deaf, blind, and feeble-minded compared. *American Annals of the Deaf, 75,* 239–240.

Berliner, D. C., & Biddle, B. J. (1995). *The manufactured crisis: Myths, fraud, and the attack on America's public schools.* New York, NY: Perseus.

Bial, R. (1999). *The on-room school.* Boston, MA: Houghton Mifflin.

Billante, J., & Hadad, C. (2010). Study: White and black children biased toward lighter skin. Retrieved from http://edition.cnn.com.

Biography. (2014). Thurgood Marshall. Retrieved from https://www.biography.com.

Black, F. (2003). *War against the weak: Eugenics and America's campaign to create a master race.* New York, NY: Avalon.

Black, R. S. (2010). Can underidentification affect exceptional learners? In F. E. Obiakor, J. P. Bakken, & A. F. Rotatori (Eds.), *Current issues and trends in special education: Identification, assessment, and instruction* (Vol. 19, pp. 37–52). Bingley, UK: Emerald.

Bloom, B. S. (Ed.), Englehart, M. D., Furst, E. J., Hill, W. H., & Karthwohl, D. R. (1956). *Taxonomy of educational goals: The classification of educational goals, handbook 1, cognitive domain.* New York, NY: David McKay.

Blount, J. M. (2002). Ella Flagg Young and the Chicago schools. In A. R. Sadovnik & S. F. Semel (Eds.), *Founding mothers and others: Women educational leaders during the progressive era* (pp. 163–176). New York, NY: Palgrave Macmillan.

Bringuier, J. (1980). *Conversations with Piaget.* Chicago, IL: University of Chicago Press.

Burch, S., & Sutherland, I. (2006). Who's not here yet? American disability history. *Radical History Review, 94,* 127–147.

Burman, E. (2008). *Deconstructing developmental psychology* (2nd ed.). London, UK: Routledge.
Bushaw, W. J. (2014). Investing in teachers: It's what Americans support. *Phi Delta Kappa, 96*(2), 52–59.
CAEP (2018). Council for the Accreditation of Educator Preparation—Accredited Provider and Recognized Programs. Retrieved from www.ncate.org/provider.
Campbell, J. (1968). *Creative mythology: The mask of god.* New York, NY: Penguin.
Campbell, J. (2008). *The hero with a thousand faces* (3rd ed.). Novato, CA: New World Library.
Chapman, L. H. (2016, February 11). Laura H. Chapman on Gates' efforts to "transform" teacher training. Retrieved from https://deutsch29.wordpress.com.
Chomsky, N. (2012). *Manufactured consent: Thought control in a democratic society.* Retrieved from http://www.youtube.com.
Chomsky, N. (2015). *Propaganda and the public mind: Interviews by David Barsamian.* Chicago, IL: Haymarket.
Chomsky, N. (2017). *Requiem for the American dream: The 10 principles of concentration of wealth and power* (Based on the film *Requiem for the American Dream*. Created and edited by P. Hutchison, K. Nyks, & J. P. Scott). New York, NY: Seven Stories Press.
Christensen, L. M., & Aldridge, J. (2013). *Critical pedagogy for early childhood and elementary educators.* New York, NY: Springer.
Clark, M. P. (1983). Mamie Phipps Clark. In A. M. O'Connell and N. F. Russo (Eds.), *Models of achievement: Reflections of eminent women in psychology* (pp. 267–277). New York, NY: Columbia University Press.
Clifford, V. (2011). Moving from multicultural to intercultural education in Australian higher education. In C. Grant & A. Portera (Eds.), *Intercultural and multicultural education: Enhancing global interconnectedness* (pp. 315–323). New York, NY: Routledge.
Collins, D. E. (1977). *Paulo Freire: His life, works and thought.* New York, NY: Paulist Press.
Cook, S., Sheerin, F., Bancel, S., & Rodrigues Gomes, J. (2012). Curriculum meeting points: A transcultural and transformative initiative in nursing education. *Nurse Education in Practice, 12*(6), 304–309.
Copple, C., & Bredekamp, S. (Eds.). (2009). *Developmentally appropriate practice in early childhood programs serving children from birth through age 8* (3rd ed.). Washington, DC: National Association for the Education of Young Children.
Crain, W. (2000). *Theories of development: Concepts and applications* (4th ed.). Upper Saddle River, NJ: Prentice Hall.
Crain, W., & Fite, K. E. (2013). Maria Montessori: Advocate for tapping into the natural curiosities of children. In J. Kirylo (Ed.), *A critical pedagogy of resistance: 34 pedagogues we need to know* (pp. 105–108). Rotterdam, Netherlands: Sense.
D'Antonio, M. (2004). *The state boys rebellion.* New York, NY: Simon & Schuster.
Darling-Hammond, L. (2006). *Powerful teacher education: Lessons from exemplary programs.* San Francisco, CA: Jossey-Bass.

Darling-Hammond, L. (2010a). Teacher education and the American future. *Journal of Teacher Education, 61*(1–2), 35–47.

Darling-Hammond, L. (2010b). *The flat world and education: How America's commitment to equity will determine our future.* New York, NY: Teachers College Press.

Darling-Hammond, L. (2010c). What we can learn from Finland's successful school reform. *NEA Today.* Retrieved from http://www.nea.org.

Darling-Hammond, L. (n.d.). Interview with Linda Darling-Hammond. PBS Online. Only a Teacher: Teachers Today. Retrieved from http://www.pbs.org.

Darling-Hammond, L., & Rothman, R. (2011). Lessons learned from Finland, Ontario, and Singapore. In L. Darling-Hammond & R. Rothman (Eds.), *Teacher and leader effectiveness in high-performing education systems* (pp. 1–11). Washington, DC: Alliance for Excellent Education.

Darling-Hammond, L., Wei, R. C., & Andree, A. (2010, August). How high-achieving countries develop great teachers. In *Stanford Center for Opportunity Policy in Education: Research brief* (pp. 1–8). Stanford, CA: Stanford Center for Opportunity Policy in Education. Retrieved from https://edpolicy.stanford.edu/sites/default/files/publications/how-high-achieving-countries-develop-great-teachers.pdf.

Darville, S. (2017). Secretary Betsy DeVos on first school visit: "Teachers are waiting to be told what they have to do." Chalkbeat. Retrieved from https://www.chalkbeat.org.

Delpit, L. (1995). *Other people's children: Cultural conflict in the classroom.* New York, NY: New Press.

Dewey, J. (1933). *How we think.* Boston, MA: D.C. Heath.

Dewey, J. (1938). *Experience and education.* New York, NY: Free Press.

Dewey, J. (1943). *The school and society* (Rev. ed.). Chicago, IL: University of Chicago Press.

Dewey, J. (1964). My pedagogic creed. In R. D. Archambault (Ed.), *John Dewey on education: Selected writings* (pp. 427–439). New York, NY: Modern Library.

Dewey, J. (1983). The Middle Works of John Dewey, 1899–1924 (Vol. 14: 1922) (J. A. Boydston, Ed.). Carbondale, IL: Southern Illinois University Press.

Edelsky, C. (1999). *Making justice our project.* Urbana, IL: National Council for Teachers of English.

Elshtain, J. B. (2002). *Jane Addams and the dream of American democracy: A life.* New York, NY: Basic Books.

Essenhigh, R. H. (2000). Letter to the editor: A few thoughts on the difference between education and training. *National Forum: The Phi Kappa Phi Journal,* p. 46.

Fee, E. (1986). Critiques of modern science: The relationship of feminism to other radical epistemologies. In R. Bleier (Ed.), *Feminist approaches to science.* Oxford, UK: Pergamon.

Families USA. (2018, July). Federal poverty guidelines. Retrieved from http://familiesusa.org.

Feiman-Nemser, S. (1990). Teacher preparation: Structural and conceptual alternatives. In W. R. Houston, M. Haberman, & J. Sikula (Eds.), *Handbook of research on teacher education: A project of the Association of Teacher Educators* (pp. 212–233). New York, NY: Macmillan.

Fischetti, J. C. (2013, January/February). Last stand for teacher education. *Childhood Education, 89*(1), 40–41.

Fischetti, J. C., & Kirylo, J. D. (2015). The looting of the American Dream: The post-Katrina rubble of public education in Louisiana. In L. Mirón, B. R. Beabout, & J. L. Boselovic (Eds.), *Only in New Orleans: School choice and equity post-hurricane Katrina* (pp. 277–284). Rotterdam, Netherlands: Sense.

Fischetti, J. (2018) Reframing teacher education for learning equity, Peabody Journal of Education, *93*(3), 267-271, DOI: 10.1080/0161956X.2018.1469228

Flexner, A. (1910). *Medical education in the United States and Canada: A report to the Carnegie foundation for the advancement of teaching.* Bulletin 4. Boston, MA: D. B. Updike, Merrymount Press.

Fraser, N. (1997). *Justice interruptus: Critical reflections on the "postsocialist" condition.* New York, NY: Routledge.

Freire, P. (1985). *The politics of education: Culture, power, and liberation.* New York, NY: Bergin & Garvey.

Freire, P. (1990). *Pedagogy of the oppressed.* New York, NY: Continuum.

Freire, P. (1994). *Education for critical consciousness.* New York, NY: Continuum.

Freire, P. (1997). *Pedagogy of the heart* (Donald Macedo & A. Oliveira, Trans.). New York, NY: Continuum International.

Freire, P. (1998). *Pedagogy of freedom: Ethics, democracy, and civic courage.* Lanham, MD: Rowman & Littlefield.

Freud, S. (1935). *New introductory lectures on psychoanalysis.* New York, NY: Norton.

Fuchs, D., & Fuchs, L. (2006). Introduction to response to intervention: What, why and how valid is it? *Reading Research Quarterly, 41*(1), 92–99.

Fuchs, D., Fuchs, L., Compton, D., Bouton, B., Caffrey, E., & Hill, L. (2007). Dynamic assessment as responsiveness to intervention: A scripted protocol to identify young at-risk readers. *Teaching Exceptional Children, 39*(5), 58–63.

Gadotti, M. (1994). *Reading Paulo Freire: His life and work* (John Milton, Trans.) (pp. 1–204). Albany, NY: State University of New York Press.

Gardner, H. (2008). *Multiple intelligences: New horizons.* New York, NY: Basic Books.

Gesell, A. (1950). *The first five years of life: A guide to the study of the pre-school child.* London, UK: Methuen.

Giordano, G. (2007). *American special education: A history of early political advocacy.* New York, NY: Peter Lang.

Giroux, H. A. (1988). *Teachers as intellectuals: Toward a critical pedagogy of learning.* South Hadley, MA: Bergin & Garvey.

Goldman, R. (2007). Teaching as transmission. In J. Aldridge & R. Goldman (Eds.), *Moving toward transformation: Teaching and learning in inclusive classrooms* (pp. 11–18). Birmingham, AL: Seacoast.

Goldman, R., Aldridge, J., & Camp, D. (2008). *A little book on theories of development: Applying theories of development to inclusive classrooms.* Birmingham, AL: Seacoast.

Gollnick, D. M., & Chinn, P. C. (2013). *Multicultural education in a pluralistic society* (9th ed.). Boston, MA: Pearson.

Goodman, K. (2014). *What's whole in whole language in the 21st century?* New York, NY: Garn Press.

Gorski, P. C. (2000). Multicultural education for equity in our schools: A working definition. EdChange. Retrieved from http://www.edchange.org/multicultural.

Gorski, P. C. (2008). Good intentions are not enough: A decolonizing intercultural education. *Intercultural Education, 19*(6), 515–525.

Graham, M. (1910). St. John Baptist de la Salle. *The Catholic Encyclopedia*. Retrieved from http://www.newadvent.org/cathen.

Grant, C., & Brueck, S. (2011). A global invitation: Toward the expansions of dialogue, reflection and creative engagement for intercultural and multicultural education. In C. Grant & A. Portera (Eds.), *Intercultural and multicultural education: Enhancing global interconnectedness* (pp. 3–11). New York, NY: Routledge.

Gross, N. (2016, May 20). Professors are overwhelmingly liberal. Do universities need to change hiring practices? *Los Angeles Times*. Retrieved from http://www.latimes.com.

Gundara, J. (2011). Citizenship and intercultural education in an international and comparative context. In C. Grant & A. Portera (Eds.), *Intercultural and multicultural education: Enhancing global interconnectedness* (pp. 294–314). New York, NY: Routledge.

Guthrie, R. (1990). Mamie Phipps Clark (1917–1983). In A. N. O'Connell and N. F. Russo (Eds.), *Women in psychology: A bio-bibliographic sourcebook*. New York, NY: Greenwood Press.

Gutmann, A. (1999). *Democratic education*. Princeton, NJ: Princeton University Press.

Guyton, E., & McIntyre, D. J. (1990). Student teaching and school experiences. In W. R. Houston, M. Haberman, & J. Sikula (Eds.), *Handbook of research on teacher education: A project of the Association of Teacher Educators* (pp. 514–534). New York, NY: Macmillan.

Hafferty, F. W., & Castellani, B. (2010). The increasing complexities of professionalism. *Academic Medicine, 85*(2), 288–301.

Hancock, L. (2005, March/April). How are the kids? *Columbia Journalism Review, 43*(6), 22–28.

Hargreaves, A., & Lo, L. (2000). The paradoxical profession: Teaching at the turn of the century. *Prospects, 30*(2), 1–16.

Harper, C., Platt, E., Naranjo, C., & Boynton, S. (2007). Marching in unison: Florida ESL teachers and No Child Left Behind. *TESOL Quarterly, 41*(3), 642–652.

Harper, V. (2014, April). Henry A. Giroux: Neoliberalism, democracy and the university as a public sphere (Interview). Truthout. Retrieved from http://www.truth-out.org.

Heafner, T., McIntyre, E., & Spooner, M. (2014). The CAEP standards and research on education preparation programs: Linking clinical partnerships with program impact. *Peabody Journal of Education, 89*(4), 516–532.

Herbst, J. (1989). *And sadly teach*. Madison, WI: University of Wisconsin Press.

Hill, B. V. (1992). Transcultural education: A model for expatriate education. *International Journal of Christianity and Education, 5*(1), 29–48.

Hinshaw, S. P. (1994). *Attention deficit hyperactivity in children*. Thousand Oaks, CA: Sage.

Hu-DeHart, E. (1993, September). The history, development, and future of ethnic studies. *Phi Delta Kappan, 75*(1), 50–54.

Honneth, A. (2003). *Redistribution or recognition? A political-philosophical exchange.* New York, NY: Verso.

Humphrey, D., Wechsler, M., & Hough, H. (2008). Characteristics of effective alternative teacher certification programs. *Teachers College Record, 110*(1), 1–63.

Jalongo, M. R. (1999). *Resisting the pendulum swing: Informed perspectives on education controversies.* Olney, MD: Association for Childhood Education International.

Jensen, M. R., Feuerestein, R., Rand, Y., Kaniel, S., & Tzuriel, D. (1988). Cultural difference and cultural deprivation: A theoretical framework for differential intervention. In R. Gupta & P. Coxhead (Eds.), *Cultural diversity and learning efficiency* (pp. 64–88). London, UK: Palgrave Macmillan.

Jungck, S., & Marshall, J. D. (1992). Curricular perspectives on one great debate. In S. Kessler & B. B. Swadener (Eds.), *Reconceptualizing the early childhood curriculum: Beginning the dialogue* (pp. 93–102). New York, NY: Teachers College Press.

Kaestle, C. F. (2008). *Victory of the common school movement: A turning point in American educational history.* Retrieved from https://publications.america.gov.

Kamii, C. (2000). *Young children reinvent arithmetic: Implications of Piaget's theory* (2nd ed.). New York, NY: Teachers College Press.

Kaplan, J. (Ed.). *Familiar quotations: A collection of passages, phrases, and proverbs traced to their sources in ancient and modern literature* (16th ed.). Boston, MA: Little, Brown.

Karger, D. (2016). Why do some universities prefer to recruit their own Ph.D. students as professors when the best candidate often comes from another school? Quora. Retrieved from https://www.quora.com.

Katz, L., & Chard. S. (2000). *Engaging children's minds: The project approach* (2nd ed.). Stamford, CT: Ablex.

Kelderman, E. (2014, November). The plight of the public regional college. *Chronicle of Higher Education.* Retrieved from http://chronicle.com.

Kilpatrick, W. H. (1918). *The project method: The use of the purposeful act in the educative process.* New York, NY: Teachers College.

Kincheloe, J. L., Slattery, P., & Steinberg, S. R. (2000). *Contextualizing teaching: Introduction to education and educational foundations.* New York, NY: Addison Wesley Longman.

King, J., & Darling-Hammond, L. (2018, May 28). Opinion: We're not doing enough to support teachers of color. *Hechinger Report.* Retrieved from http://hechingerreport.org.

Kirylo, J. D. (2011). *Paulo Freire: The man from Recife.* New York, NY: Peter Lang.

Kirylo, J. D. (2016a, November 16). Essay review of *Pedagogy of insurrection: From Resurrection to revolution*, by P. McLaren. *Education Review, 23.* http://dx.doi.org/10.14507/er.v23.2104.

Kirylo, J. D. (2016b). *Teaching with purpose: An inquiry into the who, why, and how we teach.* Lanham, MD: Rowman & Littlefield.

Kirylo, J. D. (2017). An overview of multicultural education in the USA: Grandest social experiment. *Social Studies Research and Practice, 12*(3), 354–357. https://doi.org/10.1108/SSRP-06-2017-0029.

Kirylo, J. D., & Nauman, A. (2006). The depersonalization of education and the language of accountability: A view from a local newspaper. *Journal of Curriculum and Pedagogy*, (3)1, 187–206.

Knight, L. W. (2010). *Jane Addams: Spirit in action*. New York, NY: Norton.

Koch, J. (2009). *So you want to be a teacher? Teaching and learning in the 21st century*. Boston, MA: Houghton Mifflin.

Kohn, A. (2000). *The case against standardized testing: Raising the scores, ruining the schools*. Portsmouth, NH: Heinemann.

Korthagen, F. (2001). *The pedagogy of realistic teacher education*. Mahwah, NJ: Lawrence Erlbaum.

Korthagen, F. (2004). In search of the essence of a good teacher: Towards a more holistic approach to teacher education. *Teaching and Teacher Education, 20*(1), 77–97.

Kozol, J. (2005). Still separate, still unequal: America's educational apartheid. *Harper's Magazine, 311*(1864), 41–54.

Kozol, J. (2009). *On being a teacher*. Oxford, England: Oneworld Publications.

Kymlicka, W. (1989). Liberal individualism and liberal neutrality. *Ethics, 99*(4), 883–905.

Labaree, D. F. (2008). An uneasy relationship: The history of teacher education in the university. In M. Cochran-Smith, S. Feiman-Nemser, D. J. McIntyre, & K. E. Demers (Eds.), *Handbook of research on teacher education: Enduring questions in changing contexts* (3rd ed.; pp. 290–306). New York, NY: Routledge, Taylor & Francis, Association of Teacher Educators.

Ladson-Billings, G. (1994). *The dreamkeepers: Successful teachers of African American children*. San Francisco, CA: Jossey-Bass.

Lagemann, E. C. (2000). *An elusive science: The troubling history of education research*. Chicago, IL: University of Chicago Press.

Lakoff, G. (2004). *Don't think of an elephant: Know your values and frame the debate*. White River Junction, VT: Chelsea Green.

Lasonen, J. (2011). Multiculturalism in the Nordic countries. In C. Grant & A. Portera (Eds.), *Intercultural and multicultural education: Enhancing global interconnectedness* (pp. 261–278). New York, NY: Routledge.

Lear, J. (1965). Who should govern medicine? *Saturday Review, 48*(23), 39–42.

Levin, C., Pinto, M., McCarthy, S., Moore, A., Scott, C. (n.d.). Only a teacher (1772 to late 18th century). Retrieved from http://www.pbs.org.

Levine, A. (2006). *Educating school teachers*. Washington, DC: Education Schools Project.

Lewis, C. M., & Lewis, J. R. (Eds.). (2009). *Jim Crow America: A documentary history*. Fayetteville, AR: University of Arkansas Press.

Lickey, C., & Powers, D. (2011). *Starting with their strengths: Using the project approach in early childhood special education*. New York, NY: Teachers College Press.

Lincoln, Y. S., & Guba, E. G. (1985). *Naturalistic inquiry*. Newbury Park, CA: Sage.

Locke, J. (1690). *An essay concerning human understanding*. Adelaide, South Australia: University of Adelaide Library. Retrieved from https://ebooks.adelaide.edu.au.

Longstreet, W., & Shane, H. G. (1993). *Curriculum for a new millennium*. Boston, MA: Allyn & Bacon.

Louisiana Department of Education (2011, Apr. 6) State superintendent announces choice for RSD superintendent. Retrieved from: https://www.louisianabelieves.com/newsroom/news-releases/2011/04/06/state-superintendent-announces-choice-for-rsd-superintendent.
Ludmerer, K. M. (2010). Commentary: Understanding the Flexner Report. *Academic Medicine, 8*(2), 193–196.
Lynch, E., & Hanson, M. (2011). *Developing cross-cultural competence: A guide for working with children and their families* (4th ed.). Baltimore, MD: Paul H. Brookes.
Lynch, K., & Baker, J. (2005). Equality in education: An equality of condition perspective. *Theory and Research in Education, 3,* 131–164.
Mann, R. (2007). *When freedom would triumph: The civil rights struggle in congress, 1954–1968.* Baton Rouge, LA: Louisiana State University Press.
Manning, M. L. (2002). *Developmentally appropriate middle level schools* (2nd ed.). Olney, MD: Association for Childhood Education International.
Marsh, C. J., & Willis, G. (2007). *Curriculum: Alternative approaches, ongoing issues* (4th ed.). Upper Saddle River, NJ: Pearson Education.
McDonald, M. (2003). The integration of social justice: Reshaping teacher education (PhD diss.). Stanford University, Stanford, CA.
McLean, J. (2005). Mamie Phipps Clark. In D. C. Hine (Ed.), *Black women in America* (Vol. 1; 2nd ed.; pp. 257–59). New York, NY: Oxford University Press.
Meier, D. (1995). *The power of their ideas: Lessons for American for a small school in Harlem.* Boston, MA: Beacon.
Merriam-Webster's Collegiate Dictionary (11th ed.). (2012). Springfield, MA: Merriam-Webster.
Metz, H. C. (Ed.). (1990). *Egypt: A country study.* Washington, DC: Government Printing Office for the Library of Congress. Retrieved from http://countrystudies.us.
Miller, M., & Petriwskyj, A. (2013). New directions in intercultural early education in Australia. *International Journal of Early Childhood, 45*(2), 251–266.
Mitchell, L. S. (1916). *Young geographers.* New York, NY: Bank Street College.
Mitchell, L. S. (1953). *Two lives: The story of Wesley Clair Mitchell and myself.* New York, NY: Simon & Schuster.
Monbiot, G. (2016, April 15). Neoliberalism: The ideology at the root of all our problems. *Guardian.* Retrieved from https://www.theguardian.com.
Morse, T. (2000). Ten events that shaped special education's century of dramatic change. *International Journal of Educational Reform, 9*(1), 32–38.
Nager, N., & Shapiro, E. (2007). *A progressive approach to the education of teachers: Some principles from Bank Street College of Education.* New York, NY: Bank Street College of Education.
National Association for the Advancement of Colored People (NAACP). (n.d.). Nation's premier civil rights organization. Retrieved from http://www.naacp.org.
National Institute for Excellence in Teaching (NIET). (n.d.). Our mission. Retrieved from http://www.niet.org.
Nauman, A. K. (2010). A historical overview of curriculum (Prehistory to 1900 CE). In J. D. Kirylo & A. K. Nauman (Eds.), *Curriculum development: Perspectives from*

around the world (pp. 17–30). Olney, MD: Association for Childhood Education International.

Newton, P., & Miah, M. (2017). Evidence-based higher education: Is the learning styles "myth" important? *Frontiers in Psychology, 8*, 444. doi:10.3389/fpsyg.2017.00444.

Nichols, S. (2018, May 17). Why teachers are walking out. Known.blog. Retrieved from https://sethnichols.wordpress.com.

Noll, J. (2004). *Taking sides: Clashing views on controversial educational issues*. Guilford, CT: McGraw-Hill, Dushkin.

North, C. E. (2006). More than words? Delving into the substantive meaning(s) of "social justice" in education. *Review of Educational Research, 76*(4), 507–535.

North, C. E. (2008). What is all this talk about "social justice"? Mapping the terrain of education's latest catchphrase. *Teachers College Record, 110*(6), 1182–1206.

Ober, J. (2003). Gadfly on trial: Socrates as citizen and social critic. In C. W. Blackwell (Ed.), *Dēmos: Classical Athenian democracy*. Retrieved from http://www.stoa.org.

Oliva, P. F. (2009). *Developing the curriculum* (7th ed.). Boston, MA: Pearson.

Olson, J. L., & Larson, R. G. (1965). Culturally deprived kindergarten children. Association of Supervision and Curriculum Development. Retrieved from http://www.ascd.org.

Ornstein, A. C., & Hunkins, F. P. (2004). *Curriculum: Foundations, principles, and issues* (4th ed.). Boston, MA: Allyn & Bacon.

Ozmon, H., & Craver, S. (1990). *Philosophical foundations of education* (4th ed.). Columbus, OH: Merrill.

Pai, Y., & Adler, S. A. (2001). *Cultural foundations of education* (3rd ed.). Upper Saddle River, NJ: Merrill Prentice Hall.

Paul, R. & Elder, L. (1997, April). Socratic thinking. Foundation for Critical Thinking. Retrieved from http://www.criticalthinking.org.

Peterson, K., & Kolb, D. A. (2017). *How you learn is how you live*. Oakland, CA: Barrett-Koehler.

Pinar, W., & Grumet, M. R. (1976). *Toward a poor curriculum*. Dubuque, IA: Kendall/Hunt.

Pinar, W., Reynolds, W., Slattery, P., & Taubman, P. (1995). *Understanding curriculum*. New York, NY: Peter Lang.

Portera, A. (2011). Intercultural and multicultural education: Epistemological and semantic aspects. In C. Grant & A. Portera (Eds.), *Intercultural and multicultural education: Enhancing global interconnectedness* (pp. 12–30). New York, NY: Routledge.

Ramazanoglu, C., & Holland, J. (2002). *Feminist methodology: Challenges and choices*. Thousand Oaks, CA: Sage.

Rand Corporation. (2012). Teachers matter. Retrieved from https://www.rand.org.

Rathus, S. A. (2013). *Introduction to lifespan*. Belmont, CA: Wadsworth.

Ravitch, D. (2012a, May 24). What is NCTQ (and why you should know). *Washington Post*. Retrieved from https://www.washingtonpost.com.

Ravitch, D. (2012b, June 18). Is Louisiana the worst? Retrieved from http://dianeravitch.net.

Ravitch, D. (2017, September 10). Tim Slekar: Scott Walker continues his crusade to eliminate the teaching profession. Retrieved from https://dianeravitch.net.

Rawls, J. (2001). *Justice as fairness: A restatement*. Cambridge, MA: Belknap Press of Harvard University.

Reyna, V. (2004). Why scientific research? The importance of evidence in changing educational practice. In P. McCardle & V. Chhabra (Eds.), *The voice of evidence in reading research* (pp. 47–58). Baltimore, MD: Paul H. Brookes.

Riessman, F. (1962). *Culturally deprived child*. New York, NY: Joanna Cotler Books.

Riessman, F. (1963). The culturally deprived child: A new view. *Research in Review*. Association for Supervision and Curriculum Development. Retrieved from http://www.ascd.org.

Robelen, E. W. (2005, August 19). Spellings' resume brings new twist to secretary post. *Education Week*.

Roberts, P. (2000). *Education, literacy, and humanization: Exploring the work of Paulo Freire*. Westport, CT: Bergin & Garvey.

Roediger, H. L., & Pyc, M. A. (2012). Inexpensive techniques to improve education: Applying cognitive psychology to enhance educational practice. *Journal of Applied Research in Memory and Cognition, 1*(4), 242–248.

Rose, M. (2014). Is teacher education a disaster? In V. Strauss, *The Washington Post*. Retrieved from https://www.washingtonpost.com/news/answer-sheet/wp/2014/01/13/is-teacher-education-really-a-disaster/?utm_term=.b6bd7942723e.

Sahlberg, P. (2009, April). A short history of educational reform in Finland. Retrieved from http://www.disal.it.

Sahlberg, P. (2011). The professional educator: Lessons from Finland. *American Educator, 35*(2), 34–38.

Sahlberg, P. (2012). What the U.S. can't learn from Finland about ed reform. *Washington Post*. Retrieved from http://www.washingtonpost.com.

Salend, S., & Duhaney, L. (2011). Changes in the education of students with exceptionalities. In A. F. Rotatori, F. E. Obiakor, & J. P. Bakken (Eds.), *Advances in education*, Vol. 21, *History of special education*. Bingley, UK: Emerald.

Samuels, A., Shorter, B., & Plaut, F. (1986). *A critical dictionary of Jungian analysis*. New York, NY: Routledge.

Sandall, S., Hemmeter, M., Smith, B., & McLean, M. (2005). *DEC recommended practices: A comprehensive guide for practical application in early intervention/early childhood special education* (2nd ed.). Longmont, CO: Sopris West.

Santoro, D. A. (2018). *Demoralized: Why teachers leave the profession they love and how they can stay*. Cambridge, MA: Harvard Education Press.

Santrock, J. W. (2014). *Essentials of lifespan development* (4th ed.). New York, NY: McGraw-Hill.

Schechter, M. (2018, June 28). Teachers expected to get 1% raise this year. *State*, p. 1, 6A.

Sigelman, C., & Rider, E. (2018). *Lifespan human development* (9th ed.). Boston, MA: Cengage.

Skeels, H., & Dye, H. (1939). A study of the effects of differential stimulation on mentally retarded children. *Proceedings of the American Association on Mental Deficiency, 44*, 114–136.

Sladky, J. F. X. (2014, April). Jean-Baptiste de La Salle: Educator and saint. *Crises Magazine.* Retrieved from http://www.crisismagazine.com.

Slattery, P. (1995). *Curriculum development in the postmodern era.* New York, NY: Garland.

Slattery, P., & Rapp, D. (2003). *Ethics and the foundation of education: Teaching convictions in a postmodern world.* Boston: Allyn & Bacon.

Solley, B. A. (2007). On standardized testing: An ACEI position paper. *Childhood Education, 84*(1), 31–37.

Sondel, B. (2013). Raising citizens or raising test scores? Teach for America and "no excuses" charter schools in post-Katrina New Orleans (PhD diss.). University of Wisconsin–Madison, Madison, WI.

Stodolsky, E., & Lesser, G. (1967). Learning patterns in the disadvantaged. *Harvard Educational Review, 37,* 546–593.

Stokes, W. T. (1997). Progressive teacher education: Consciousness, identity, and knowledge. In P. Freire, J. W. Fraser, D. Macedo, T. McKinnon, & W. T. Stokes (Eds.), *Mentoring the mentor: A critical dialogue with Paulo Freire* (pp. 201–227). New York: Peter Lang.

Strauss, V. (2013a, December 5). Why educating the educators is complex. *Washington Post.* Retrieved from https://www.washingtonpost.com.

Strauss, V. (2013b, December 16). What's right—and very wrong—with the teacher education debate. *Washington Post.* Retrieved from https://www.washingtonpost.com.

Strauss, V. (2014, January 13). Is teacher education a disaster? *Washington Post.* Retrieved from https://www.washingtonpost.com.

Strauss, V. (2015, November 23). Gates Foundation put millions of dollars into new education focus: Teacher preparation. *Washington Post.* Retrieved from https://www.washingtonpost.com.

Strauss, V. (2016, December 21). "Government really sucks" and five other principles promoted by Trump's education nominee. *Washington Post.* Retrieved from https://www.washingtonpost.com.

Strauss, V. (2017, September 24). Government, Betsy DeVos once said, "sucks." Now she's wielding its power to push her agenda. *Washington Post.* Retrieved from https://www.washingtonpost.com.

Sutcher, L., Darling-Hammond, L., & Carver-Thomas, D. (2016, September). *A coming crisis in teaching? Teacher supply, demand, and shortages in the U.S.* Palo Alto, CA: Learning Policy Institute.

Sykes, G. (2008). Teacher education and the predicament of reform. In M. Cochran-Smith, S. Feiman-Nemser, D. J. McIntyre, & K. E. Demers (Eds.), *Handbook of research on teacher education: Enduring questions in changing contexts* (3rd ed.; pp. 1294–1309). New York, NY: Routledge, Taylor & Francis Group, and the Association of Teacher Educators.

Taylor, A. H. (1976). *Travail and triumph: Black life and culture in the south since the Civil War.* Westport, CT: Greenwood Press.

Texas Tech Today (TTU). (2015). Bill and Melinda Gates Foundation. Retrieved from https://today.ttu.edu.

Tiedt, P. L., & Tiedt, I. M. (2005). *Multicultural teaching: A handbook of activities, information, and resources* (7th ed.). Boston, MA: Pearson, Allyn & Bacon.

Tye, B. (2000). *Hard truths: Uncovering the deep structure of schooling.* New York, NY: Teachers College Press.

Tyler, R. (1949). *Basic principles of curriculum and instruction.* Chicago, IL: University of Chicago Press.

U.S. Department of Education. (2002). *Meeting the highly qualified teachers challenge: The secretary's annual report on teacher quality.* Washington, DC: Author. Retrieved from https://www2.ed.gov.

U.S. National Commission on Excellence in Education. (1983). *A nation at risk: The imperative for educational reform; A report to the Nation and the Secretary of Education, United States Department of Education.* Washington, DC: Commission. Retrieved from http://www2.ed.gov.

Vygotsky, L. S. (1978). *Mind in society: The development of higher psychological processes.* Cambridge, MA: Harvard University Press.

Webb, L. D., Metha, A., & Jordan, K. F. (2007). *Foundations of American education* (5th ed.). Upper Saddle River, NJ: Pearson Education.

Wegwert, J. C., & Foley, J. A. (2017). Colleges of education and the making of the neoliberal university. In F. Mizikaci & G. Senese (Eds.), with Y. T. Cakcak & S. Gorman, *A language of freedom and teacher's authority* (pp. 53–65). Lanham, MD: Lexington Books.

Wei, R. C., Andree, A., & Darling-Hammond, L. (2009). How nations invest in teachers. *Educational Leadership, 66*(5), 28–33.

Williams, J. (1987). *Eyes on the prize: America's civil rights years, 1954–1965.* New York, NY: Penguin.

Wilson, E. O. (2014). *The meaning of human existence.* New York, NY: Liveright.

Wink, J. (2011). *Critical pedagogy: Notes from the real world* (4th ed.). Boston, MA: Pearson.

Winzer, M. (1998). A tale often told: The early progression of special education. *Remedial and Special Education, 19*(4), 212–218.

Wulf, C. (2010). Education a transcultural education: A global challenge. *Educational Studies in Japan International Yearbook, 5*, 33–47.

Yatvin, J. (2003). Science means what we say it means, or, my adventures in wonderland. In R. Lent & G. Pipkin (Eds.), *Silent no more: Voices of courage in American schools* (pp. 33–43). Portsmouth, NH: Heinemann.

Young, E. F. (1901). *Isolation in the school.* Chicago, IL: University of Chicago Press.

Young, I. M. (1990). *Justice and the politics of difference.* Princeton, NJ: Princeton University Press.

Zemelman, S., Daniels, H., & Hyde, A. (1998). *Best practice: New standards for teaching and learning in America's schools* (2nd ed.). Portsmouth, NH: Heinemann.

Index

aboriginal/indigenous studies programs, 14
academic freedom, xi
accountability: reform, compromising K-12 education, and, 21–25; with transaction learning, 76
accrediting agencies, two-stepping among, 57–59
acculturation, 84
activism matters, xiii, 16–17
Addams, Jane, 16; educational contributions of, 9; Hull House opened by, 9
administration, 27–28, 53–54, 66
African Americans, 3, 11, 12, 82
American Civil Liberties Union, 9
Anthony, Susan B., 3
apartheid, 3
Apology (Plato), 4
approaches, to curricula, 69, 70, 71
autonomy, independence and, 81

Bank Street College of Education, 10, 54, 58, 70, 75
BEA. *See* Bilingual Education Act
BEE. *See* Bureau of Educational Experiments
behaviorism, 79, 80

behavior problems, family to blame for, 80
Berliner, David, 22
BESE. *See* Louisiana Board of Elementary and Secondary Education
Best Practices Center (BPC), x, 33
Biddle, Bruce, 22
Bilingual Education Act (BEA) in 1968, 12
Black-ish, 85
blended instruction, 91–93
The Blob, 34–35
BPC. *See* Best Practices Center
Bringuier, Jean-Claude, 81
broken schools, 21–22
Brown v Topeka Board of Education, 11, 12, 18n4
Bureau of Educational Experiments (BEE), 10
Bush, George W., 23, 26n2, 53–54
business-model approach, to teacher education programs, 62

CAEP. *See* Council for the Accreditation of Educator Preparation
Campbell, Joseph, 86

Carver, George Washington, 3
certification degrees, for teachers, 41
child-centered philosophy of education, of Rousseau, 5–6
child development, universal stages of, 80–81
Chomsky, N., 29, 30n3
Chronicle of Higher Education, 42
civil rights: of African Americans, 3; in education, 12–13
code switching, 84–85
colleges of education: emergence of, 41–42; two-stepping among, 57–59
commercialism, in "Flexner Report," 102
common schools, 6–7, 39, 40
compensation, hiring process and, 45–46; disparity with, 49, 51n1; diversity with, 50; external sameness/difference with, 50; ideological sameness/difference with, 50–51; market value impact on, 49; politics and philosophies relating to, 50
competition, knowledge base and, ix
concentric beliefs, about curriculum and instruction, 66
conceptions, of transformation learning, 76
conscientização (conscientization), 15–16
constructivist approach, of transaction learning, 74
content, methods versus, 66
Council for the Accreditation of Educator Preparation (CAEP), 54, 55, 57–58
critical thinking, of Socrates, 4–5
culturally deprived student, 82
cultures, 79; acculturation, 84; conflicts with, 86; hybrid, 85–86; intercultural education, 83–84, 86; interculturalism, 82; multicultural education, 13–14, 82–86; multiculturalism, 82, 83; transcendent culturing, 84; transcultural education, 84–87;

transculturalism, 82; transferential culturing, 84–85; variations of, 86
curriculum, xiii; approaches to, 69, 70, 71; fidelity of treatment relating to, 69; frameworks for, 69, 71; here and now, 55; models of, 69–70, 71
curriculum, instruction and: administration with, 66; concentric beliefs about, 66; content, methods versus, relating to, 66; cyclical notions of, 66; dualistic conception of, 65; interlocking conception of, 66; pedagogy relating to, 65, 67n2; teaching methods relating to, 65; Tylerian model with, 65, 67n1
cyclical notions, of curriculum and instruction, 66

dame schools, 39
Darling-Hammond, L., xiv, 104–5, 106n5
Department of Education, U.S., 54
development: without context, 80–81; diversity or human, 13–14, 79–86
Developmental-Interaction approach, 70
developmental psychology, 67
DeVos, Betsy, ix, 25, 27, 32
Dewey, John, 16, 23, 103; personal disposition and, 8; progressive education movement by, 7, 102; teacher as professional cultivated by, 8; University Laboratory School at University of Chicago founded by, 8
Discovery Doctrine, 13
disparity, with compensation and hiring process, 49, 51n1
distraction, in moving forward: problems relating to, 98; public fickleness relating to, 99–100; Rose on, 97–98, 100n2; solutions for, 98; Strauss on, 97, 100n1; teacher role as paradoxical, 99–100

diversity: with compensation and hiring process, 50; human development or, 13–14, 79–87
Dropbox, 92
dualistic conception, of curriculum and instruction, 65
DuBois, W. E. B., 11

economic change, ix
edTPA, 59
education, 5; civil rights in, 12–13; colleges of, 41–42, 57–59; history of, xiii; intercultural, 83–84, 86; K-12, 21–25, 54; Mann as father of, 6; Mitchell as pioneer in, 10; multicultural, 13–14, 82–84, 86; philosophies of, x; progressive movement of, 7, 102; public, as doing poorly, 28–29; special, 45, 67; training and, 104–5, 106n5; transcultural, 84–87. *See also* teacher education
education, teacher, ix–xiii, 7; hierarchy of, 103; programs for, 61–62; rocky historical road toward, 39, 42, 42n1, 42n3; traditional, elimination of, 31–35, 35nn1–4, 36n12
educational contributions: of Addams, 9; of Young, 9
Education for all Handicapped Children Act, 12
education narrative, hijacking of, 34–35
education theory, fast-track programs and, x
"enantiodromia is a psychological law," 87
entrance requirements, in "Flexner Report," 102
equality opportunity access, to teacher education programs, 61
Essenhigh, Robert H., 104
ethnic studies, aboriginal/indigenous studies programs and, 14
external sameness/difference, 50

facilitated freedom approach, of Montessori, 10–11
faculty expectations, 45–46
family, behavior problems blamed on, 80
fast-track programs, toward certification, 27; advent of, x; educational theory minimized by, x; on the job learning with, x; pedagogy minimized by, x; philosophies of education minimized by, x
father: of education, Mann as, 6; of Western philosophy, Socrates as, 5
Father Knows Best, 85
fidelity of treatment, curricula relating to, 69
Fischetti, John, 97, 98
Flexner, Abraham, xiii, 101–2; Dewey influence on, 103
"Flexner-like" moment, xiii, 101–3; training, education and, 104–5, 106n5; turning point with, 105
"Flexner Report": buggy reference with, 103, 106n1; commercialism with, 102; entrance requirements with, 102; findings of, 101; public attention with, 102; recommendations with, 102
frameworks, for curricula, 69, 71
Fraser, Nancy, model of social justice of, 45–48, 48n1
free market advocates, ix
Freire, Paulo, xii, 17, 34, xivn3; *conscientização* concept of, 15–16; *Pedagogy of the Oppressed* by, 15; philosophy of, 15
Froebel, Friedrich Wilhelm, 7, 11

Gates, Bill, 32
Gates Foundation, 32–33, 34
generative model, with transaction learning, 74
globalization, ix, 27

Great Society, 27
Gutenberg, Johannes, 3

here and now curriculum, 55
Higher Education Act, Title IX to, 12–13
history, changes in course of, 3–4, 17n1
Hull House, Addams opening of, 9
human development, diversity or: autonomy, independence and, 81; behaviorism, 79, 80; blaming family, 80; constructivism, 79; courses for, 79; culture relating to, 79, 82; development without context, 80–81; intercultural education, 83–84, 86; middle-class bias, 80; multicultural education, 13–14, 82–83; prescribed instruction, 81–82; theories about, 79–80, 81; transcultural education, 84–87
hybrid cultures, 85–86

IDEA. *See* Individuals with Disabilities Education Improvement Act of 2004
ideological sameness/difference, 50–51
IEPs. *See* individualized education programs
independence, 81
individualized education programs (IEPs), 12
Individuals with Disabilities Education Improvement Act of 2004 (IDEA), 45
instruction: blended, 91–93; curriculum and, 65–66, 67n1, 67n2; prescribed, 81–82; total in-class, 89–90; total online, 90–91
intercultural education: background of, 83; multicultural education and, 83–84, 86; terms associated with, 83
interculturalism, 82
interlocking conception, of curriculum and instruction, 66
Isolation in the School (Young), 9

"Is Teacher Education a Disaster" (Strauss), 97, 100n1

Jim Crow South, 11
Johnson v M'Intosh, 13

K-12 education, 21–25, 54
King, Martin Luther, Jr., 3, 12
KKK, 11
knowledge base, competition and, ix

language, transmission of, 73
"Last Stand for Teacher Education" (Fischetti), 97
Lau v Nichols, 12
learning: on the job, x; styles of, with sameness, difference versus, 46; transaction, 7, 74–76; transformation, 76–78, 85; transmission, 73–74
Leave It to Beaver, 85
liberal arts programs, 41
Locke, John, 5, 17n
Louisiana Board of Elementary and Secondary Education (BESE), 24

macro versus micro challenge: administrative levels, 53–54; here and now curriculum, 55; pedagogical practices in K-12 influenced by, 54; teaching practices, 54–55
Mandela, Nelson, 3
Manifest Destiny, 13
Mann, Horace, ix, 16; common school movement led by, 6–7, 39, 40; as father of education, 6; teacher education program established by, 7
Man on a Ledge, 97
The Manufactured Crises (Berliner, Biddle), 22
market value impact, on compensation and hiring process, 49
Marshall, Thurgood, 16–17; *Brown v Topeka Board of Education* and, 11,

12, 18n4; NAACP and, 11; *Plessy v Ferguson* and, 11
materials, with transaction learning, 75
McQueen, Steve, 34–35
Medical Education in the United States and Canada (Flexner), 101
middle-class bias, 80
Milken, Lowell, x, 33
Mitchell, Lucy Sprague, 16; BEE founded by, 10; as pioneer in education, 10
models: business-model approach, to teacher education programs, 62; of curricula, 69–70, 71; Fraser model of social justice, 45–48, 48n1; generative, with transaction learning, 74; Tylerian model, with curriculum and instruction, 65, 67n1
Modern Family, 85
money, elimination of traditional teacher education programs relating to, 33–34, 36n12
Montessori, Maria, 16; facilitated freedom approach of, 10–11; medical degree of, 10
multicultural education: advent of, 13–14; intercultural education and, 83–84, 86; "tossed salad" relating to, 14; tour or detour approach to, 82–83; WASP relating to, 13
multiculturalism, 82, 83

National Association for the Advancement of Colored People (NAACP), 11
National Association for the Education of Young Children, 10
National Council for Accreditation of Teacher Education (NCATE), 57
National Council on Teaching Quality (NCTQ), x, 32
National Education Association, Young as first female president of, 9

National Institute for Excellence in Teaching (NIET), x, xi, 33, 35n9
National Reading Panel, 65–66, 67
A Nation at Risk report, in 1983, 22–23, 27
NCATE. *See* National Council for Accreditation of Teacher Education
NCLB. *See* No Child Left Behind Act
NCTQ. *See* National Council on Teaching Quality
neoliberal agenda, xivn1; for outsourcing, ix; for privatization, ix
neoliberalism: definition of, 29; privatization relating to, 27; Reagan administration relating to, 27–28; systemic effort to privatize, 27–30
New Deal, 27
NIET. *See* National Institute for Excellence in Teaching
NIET Higher Education Handbook, 33
No Child Left Behind (NCLB) Act, x, 31, 45, 47; of Bush, 23, 26n2, 53–54; human development theory relating to, 81; model of, 69
normal schools, 39–41, 42n1, 42n3

Obama, Barack, 54
"Old Deluder Satan" Act, 6, 18n3
online delivery systems: blended instruction, 91–93; total in-class instruction, 89–90; total online instruction, 90–91
on the job learning, x
open-door policy, with teacher education programs, 61

Paige, Rodney, ix–x, 23, 24, xivn2
Pastorek, Paul, 24, 27
PDK. *See* Phi Delta Kappa
pedagogical approach, of Socrates, 4–5
pedagogical practices, in K-12, 54
pedagogy, x, xiii; with curriculum and instruction, 65, 67n2

performance, with reform, accountability, compromising K-12 education, 21
Pestalozzi, Johann Heinrich, 7, 11
Phi Delta Kappa (PDK) Gallup poll, in 2014, 100
philosophies: of education, x, 6; of Freire, 15; impact on, with compensation and hiring process, 50; political, 5; of Rousseau, 5, 6; Socrates relating to, 5
Piaget, Jean, 16, 79, 80, 81
Plato, 4
Plessy v Ferguson, 11
political philosophies, 5
politics: impact of, on compensation and hiring process, 50; with teacher education, xiii
PRAXIS test requirements, 58, 59
prescribed instruction, 81–82
privatization, ix, 27–30
profession, definition of, 101
programs, 7, 14, 23–25. *See also specific programs*
progressive education movement, by Dewey, 7, 102
psychology, developmental, 67
public education, as doing poorly, 28–29
public fickleness, teacher education relating to, 99–100
Public Law 94-142, 12, 18n5

quantity-versus-quality conundrum, with teacher education, xi, 61–62

Race to the Top program, 23, 54
Reagan administration, neoliberalism relating to, 27–28
recommendations, with "Flexner Report," 102
Recovery School District (RSD), 24
reform, accountability, compromising K-12 education: with broken schools, 21–22; concepts of, 21–25; mediocrity relating to, 22; performance with, 21; programs for, 23–25
research, with sameness, difference versus, 46–47, 49
resources, for transaction learning, 76
Rhee, Michelle, 25, 27
Rose, Mike, 32, 97–98, 100n2
Rousseau, Jean-Jacques, 16; child-centered philosophy of education of, 6; children and adults relating to, 5–6; political philosophy of, 5
RSD. *See* Recovery School District

sameness, difference versus: compensation and hiring process relating to, 45–46; external, 50; faculty expectations relating to, 45–46; Fraser model of social justice, 45–48, 48n1; IDEA relating to, 45; ideological, 50–51; learning styles with, 46; NCLB relating to, 45, 47; research with, 46–47, 49; service relating to, 47–48, 49; teaching, 45–48, 49
schools: of education, emergence of, 41–42; as testing centers, 29. *See also specific schools*
separate but equal, 11
service, with sameness, difference versus, 47–48, 49
social upheaval, ix
Socrates, 16; critical thinking of, 4–5; as father of Western philosophy, 5; pedagogical approach of, 4–5; Socratic method by, 4
Socratic method, 4
special education, 67; accommodations with, 45; modifications with, 45
Spellings, Margaret, 24–25, 26nn5–6, 27
Stanton, Elizabeth Cady, 3
State Departments of Education, xi, xii, 54, 55, 57–59, 61, 70

Strauss, Valerie, 97, 100n1
students, 77, 82
synergistic affect, with transformation learning, 78, 85
System for Teacher and Student Advancement (TAP), x, 33

TAP. *See* System for Teacher and Student Advancement
teacher education: academic freedom with, xi; activism relating to, xiii, 16–17; assault on, x; best preparation for, xii; criticism of, ix; external forces, xii; as formal field of study, ix; internal forces, xii; internal struggles of, xi; issues with, xii; low status of, 42; Mann establishment of program for, 7; moving forward with, xiii; politics relating to, xiii; public fickleness relating to, 99–100; quantity-versus-quality conundrum with, xi, 61–62; tenure relating to, xi; undermining of, ix; working solutions relating to, xiii
teacher education, rocky historical road toward: emergence of schools and colleges of education, 41–42; normal schools, 39–41, 42n1, 42n3
teacher education programs: business-model approach to, 62; equal opportunity access to, 61; open-door policy with, 61
teacher education programs, traditional, elimination of, 32; education narrative, hijacking of, 34–35; money relating to, 33–34, 36n12; teacher shortages relating to, 31, 35nn1–4
Teacher Preparation Transformation Centers, 32
teachers: certification degrees for, 41; in educational hierarchy, 103; marginalization of, 74; as professional, 8; as reflective decision makers, 57; shortages of, 31, 35nn1–4; transaction method with, 7; transmission by, 73–74; women employed as, 39–40, 42n2, 103
teachers, role of: paradoxical, 99–100; with transaction learning, 7; with transformation learning, 76–77
Teach for America (TFA), x, 23–25, 26n3, 32
teaching: methods of, with curriculum and instruction, 65; practices of, with macro versus micro challenge, 54–55; with sameness, difference versus, 45–48, 49
technology, for transmission learning, 73
Texas Tech-based University-School Partnerships for the Renewal of Educator Preparation Nation Center, 32
TFA. *See* Teach for America
Thorndike, Edward L., 7, 103, 106nn2–4
Tiananmen Square, 3–4
Title IX, to Higher Education Act, 12–13
total in-class instruction, 89–90
total online instruction, 90–91
tour or detour approach, to multicultural education, 82–83
trade, definition of, 101
training, education and, 104–5, 106n5
transaction learning: accountability with, 76; advantages of, 75; Bank Street approach for, 75; as constructivist approach of, 74; drawbacks to, 75; as generative model, 74; learning choices with, 74; materials with, 75; resources for, 76; teacher role with, 7
transcendence, transferential culturing relating to, 85
transcendent culturing, 84
transcultural education: challenges of, 87; definition of, 84; honor and respect relating to, 87; hybrid

cultures relating to, 85–86; tribalism relating to, 86–87
transculturalism, 82
transferential culturing: as code switching, 84–85; definition of, 84; transcendence relating to, 85
transformation learning: benefits of, 77–78; challenges of, 78; conceptions of, 76; definition of, 76; student role in, 77; synergistic affect with, 78, 85; teacher role with, 76–77
transmission learning: definition of, 73; drawbacks with, 74; of language, 73; by teachers, 73; teachers marginalized by, 74; technology for, 73
tribalism, 86–87
Tylerian model, with curriculum and instruction, 65, 67n1

University Laboratory School at University of Chicago, Dewey founding of, 8

Venn diagram, 66
Voting Rights Act of 1965, 12
Vygotsky, L. S., 79, 81

Washington Post, 97
WASP. *See* White Anglo-Saxon Protestant
welfare queens, 27, 28
White, John, 24, 27, 32
White Anglo-Saxon Protestant (WASP), 13
Winfrey, Oprah, 4
women, as teachers, 39–40, 42n2, 103
Wright, Orville, 3
Wright, Wilbur, 3

Young, Ella Flagg, 16; educational contributions of, 9; as first woman president of National Education Association, 9; *Isolation in the School* by, 9

About the Authors

James D. Kirylo is associate professor of education at the University of South Carolina. Among other books, he is author of *Teaching with Purpose: An Inquiry into the Who, Why, and How We Teach* (2016) and *Paulo Freire: The Man from Recife* (2011).

Jerry Aldridge is professor emeritus of early childhood education at the University of Alabama at Birmingham. He is author of numerous books, including Rowman & Littlefield's *Stealing from the Mother: The Marginalization of Women in Education and Psychology from 1900–2010* (2013) with Lois M. Christensen.

www.ingramcontent.com/pod-product-compliance
Lightning Source LLC
Chambersburg PA
CBHW030142240426
43672CB00005B/238